The Common Law

LIST OF ILLUSTRATIONS

PAGE

"'Dearest,' he whispered, putting his arm around her, 'you must come with us'" 427

"'Well, Louis, what do you know about this?'" 430

"The parrot greeted her, flapping his brilliant wings and shrieking from his perch" 449

"'And they—the majority of them—are, after all, just men'" . 453

"His thoughts were mostly centred on Valerie" 458

"Ogilvy . . . began a lively fencing bout with an imaginary adversary" 478

"Then Rita came silently on sandalled feet to stand behind him and look at what he had done" 483

"'You'd better understand, Kelly, that Rita Tevis is as well born as I am'" 491

"She knelt down beside the bed and . . . said whatever prayer she had in mind" 507

"She was longer over her hair . . . gathering it and bringing it under discipline" 510

"'Yes,' she said, 'it is really great'" 521

"'I am scared blue. That's why I'm holding on to your hand so desperately'" 531

THE COMMON LAW

CHAPTER I

THERE was a long, brisk, decisive ring at the door.
He continued working. After an interval the bell rang
again, briefly, as though the light touch on the electric
button had lost its assurance.

"Somebody's confidence has departed," he thought
to himself, busy with a lead-weighted string and a
stick of soft charcoal wrapped in silver foil. For a
few moments he continued working, not inclined to trouble himself to answer the door, but the hesitating timidity of a third appeal amused him, and he walked out
into the hallway and opened the door. In the dim
light a departing figure turned from the stairway:

"Do you wish a model?" she asked in an unsteady
voice.

"No," he said, vexed.

"Then—I beg your pardon for disturbing
you——"

"Who gave you my name?" he demanded.

"Why—nobody——"

"Who sent you to me? Didn't anybody send you?"

"No."

"But how did you get in?"

"I—walked in."

There was a scarcely perceptible pause; then she
turned away in the dim light of the corridor.

1

"There was a long, brisk, decisive ring at the door."

" You models have your own guild, your club, your
regular routine, and it would make it much easier for
us if you'd all register and quietly wait until we send
for you.

" You see we painters know what we want and we
know where to apply for it. But if you all go wandering over studio buildings in search of engagements, we
won't have any leisure to employ you because it will take
all our time to answer the bell. And it will end by our
not answering it at all. And that's why it is fit and
proper for good little models to remain *chez eux*."

He had achieved a point to his pencil. Now he
opened his model book, looked up at her with his absent
smile, and remained looking.

" Aren't you going to remove your veil? "

" Oh—I beg your pardon! " Slender gloved fingers
flew up, were nervously busy a moment. She removed
her veil and sat as though awaiting his comment. None
came.

After a moment's pause she said: " Did you wish—
my name and address? "

He nodded, still looking intently at her.

" Miss West," she said, calmly. He wrote it down.

" Is that all? Just ' Miss West ' ? "

" Valerie West—if that is custom—necessary."

He wrote " Valerie West "; and, as she gave it to
him, he noted her address.

" Head and shoulders? " he asked, quietly.

" Yes," very confidently.

" Figure? "

" Yes,"—less confidently.

" Draped or undraped? "

When he looked up again, for an instant he thought

"How many engagements have you? Is your time all cut up—as I fancy it is?"

"N-no."

"Could you give me what time I might require?"

"I think so."

"What I mean, Miss West, is this: suppose that your figure is what I have an idea it is; could you give me a lot of time ahead?"

She remained silent so long that he had started to write, "probably unreliable," under his notes; but, as his pencil began to move, her lips unclosed with a low, breathless sound that became a ghost of a voice:

"I will do what you require of me. I meant to answer."

"Do you mean that you are in a position to make a time contract with me?—provided you prove to be what I need?"

She nodded uncertainly.

"I'm beginning the ceiling, lunettes, and panels for the Byzantine Theatre," he added, sternly stroking his short mustache, "and under those circumstances I suppose you know what a contract between us means."

She nodded again, but in her eyes was bewilderment, and in her heart, fear.

"Yes," she managed to say, "I think I understand."

"Very well. I merely want to say that a model threw me down hard in the very middle of the Bimmington's ball-room. Max Schindler put on a show, and she put for the spot-light. She'd better stay put," he added grimly: "she'll never have another chance in your guild."

Then the frown vanished, and the exceedingly engaging smile glimmered in his eyes:

7

"You wouldn't do such a thing as that to me," he added; "would you, Miss West?"

"Oh, no," she replied, not clearly comprehending the enormity of the Schindler recruit's behaviour.

"And you'll stand by me if our engagement goes through?"

"Yes, I—will try to."

"Good business! Now, if you really are what I have an idea you are, I'll know pretty quick whether I can use you for the Byzantine job." He rose, walked over to a pair of closed folding doors and opened them. "You can undress in there," he said. "I think you will find everything you need."

For a second she sat rigid, her black-gloved hands doubled, her eyes fastened on him as though fascinated. He had already turned and sauntered over to one of several easels where he picked up the lump of charcoal in its silver foil.

The colour began to come back into her face— swifter, more swiftly: the vast blank window with its amber curtains stared at her; she lifted her tragic gaze and saw the sheet of glass above swimming in crystal light. Through it clouds were dissolving in the bluest of skies; against it a spiderweb of pendant cords drooped from the high ceiling; and she saw the looming mystery of huge canvases beside which stepladders rose surmounted by little crow's-nests where the graceful oval of palettes curved, tinted with scraped brilliancy.

"What a dreamer you are!" he called across the studio to her. "The light is fine, now. Hadn't we better take advantage of it?"

She managed to find her footing; contrived to rise,

8

to move with apparent self-possession toward the folding doors.

"Better hurry," he said, pleasantly. "If you're what I need we might start things now. I am all ready for the sort of figure I expect you have."

She stepped inside the room and became desperately busy for a moment trying to close the doors; but either her hands had suddenly become powerless or they shook too much; and when he turned, almost impatiently, from his easel to see what all that rattling meant, she shrank hastily aside into the room beyond, keeping out of his view.

The room was charming—not like the studio, but modern and fresh and dainty with chintz and flowered wall-paper and the graceful white furniture of a bedroom. There was a flowered screen there, too. Behind it stood a chair, and onto this she sank, laid her hands for an instant against her burning face, then stooped and, scarcely knowing what she was about, began to untie her patent-leather shoes.

He remained standing at his easel, very busy with his string and lump of charcoal; but after a while it occurred to him that she was taking an annoyingly long time about a simple matter.

"What on earth is the trouble?" he called. "Do you realise you've been in there a quarter of an hour?"

She made no answer. A second later he thought he heard an indistinct sound—and it disquieted him.

"Miss West?"

There was no reply.

Impatient, a little disturbed, he walked across to the folding doors; and the same low, suppressed sound caught his ear.

deep into the pink palm. She was trying to look at him. Her face was as white as a flower.

" All right," he said under his breath, " you're practically faultless. I suppose you realise it!"

A scarcely perceptible shiver passed over her entire body, then, as he stepped back, his keen artist's gaze narrowing, there stole over her a delicate flush, faintly staining her from brow to ankle, transfiguring the pallour exquisitely, enchantingly. And her small head drooped forward, shadowed by her hair.

" You're what I want," he said. " You're about everything I require in colour and form and texture."

She neither spoke nor moved as much as an eyelash.

" Look here, Miss West," he said in a slightly excited voice, " let's go about this thing intelligently." He swung another easel on its rollers, displaying a sketch in soft, brilliant colours—a multitude of figures amid a swirl of sunset-tinted clouds and patches of azure sky.

" You're intelligent," he went on with animation,— " I saw that—somehow or other—though you haven't said very much." He laughed, and laid his hand on the painted canvas beside him:

" You're a model, and it's not necessary to inform you that this is only a preliminary sketch. Your experience tells you that. But it is necessary to tell you that it's the final composition. I've decided on this arrangement for the ceiling. You see for yourself that you're perfectly fitted to stand or sit for all these floating, drifting, cloud-cradled goddesses. You're an inspiration in yourself—for the perfections of Olympus!" he added, laughing, " and that's no idle compliment. But of course other artists have often told you this before— as though you didn't have eyes of your own! And beautiful ones at that!" He laughed again, turned and dragged a two-storied model-stand across the floor, tossed up one or two silk cushions, and nodded to her.

"Don't be afraid; it's rickety but safe. It will hold us both. Are you ready?"

As in a dream she set one little bare foot on the steps, mounted, balancing with arms extended and the tips of her fingers resting on his outstretched hand.

Standing on the steps he arranged the cushions, told her where to be seated, how to recline, placed the wedges and blocks to support her feet, chalked the bases, marked positions with arrows, and wedged and blocked up her elbow. Then he threw over her a soft, white, wool robe, swathing her from throat to feet, descended the steps, touched an electric bell, and picking up a huge clean palette began to squeeze out coils of colour from a dozen plump tubes.

Presently a short, squarely built man entered. He wore a blue jumper; there were traces of paint on it, on his large square hands, on his square, serious face.

"O'Hara?"

"Sorr?"

"We're going to begin *now!*—thank Heaven. So if you'll be kind enough to help move forward the ceiling canvas——"

O'Hara glanced up carelessly at the swathed and motionless figure above, then calmly spat upon his hands and laid hold of one side of the huge canvas indicated. The painter took the other side.

"Now, O'Hara, careful! Back off a little!—don't let it sway! There—that's where I want it. Get a ladder and clamp the tops. Pitch it a little forward

"'Now, Miss West,' he said decisively."

—more!—stop! Fix those pully ropes; I'll make things snug below."

For ten minutes they worked deftly, rapidly, making fast the great blank canvas which had been squared and set with an enormous oval in heavy outline.

From her lofty eyrie she looked down at them as in a dream while they shifted other enormous framed canvases and settled the oval one into place. Everything below seemed to be on rubber wheels or casters, easels, stepladders, colour cabinets, even the great base where the oval set canvas rested.

She looked up at the blue sky. Sparrows dropped out of the brilliant void into unseen cañons far below from whence came the softened roar of traffic. Northward the city spread away between its rivers, glittering under the early April sun; the Park lay like a grey and green map set with the irregular silver of water; beyond, the huge unfinished cathedral loomed dark against the big white hospital of St. Luke; farther still a lilac-tinted haze hung along the edges of the Bronx.

" All right, O'Hara. Much obliged. I won't need you again."

" Very good, Sorr."

The short, broad Irishman went out with another incurious glance aloft, and closed the outer door.

High up on her perch she watched the man below. He calmly removed coat and waistcoat, pulled a painter's linen blouse over his curly head, lighted a cigarette, picked up his palette, fastened a tin cup to the edge, filled it from a bottle, took a handful of brushes and a bunch of cheese cloth, and began to climb up a stepladder opposite her, lugging his sketch in the other hand.

He fastened the little sketch to an upright and stood on the ladder halfway up, one leg higher than the other.

" Now, Miss West," he said decisively.

At the sound of his voice fear again leaped through her like a flame, burning her face as she let slip the white wool robe.

" All right," he said. " Don't move while I'm drawing unless you have to."

She could see him working. He seemed to be drawing with a brush, rapidly, and with a kind of assurance that appeared almost careless.

At first she could make out little of the lines. They were all dark in tint, thin, tinged with plum colour. There seemed to be no curves in them—and at first she could not comprehend that he was drawing her figure. But after a little while curves appeared; long delicate outlines began to emerge as rounded surfaces in monochrome, casting definite shadows on other surfaces. She could recognise the shape of a human head; saw it gradually become a colourless drawing; saw shoulders, arms, a body emerging into shadowy shape; saw the long fine limbs appear, the slender indication of feet.

Then flat on the cheek lay a patch of brilliant colour, another on the mouth. A great swirl of cloud forms sprang into view high piled in a corner of the canvas.

And now he seemed to be eternally running up and down his ladder, shifting it here and there across the vast white background of canvas, drawing great meaningless lines in distant expanses of the texture, then, always consulting her with his keen, impersonal gaze, he pushed back his ladder, mounted, wiped the big brushes, selected others smaller and flatter, considering her in penetrating silence between every brush stroke.

She saw a face and hair growing lovely under her eyes, bathed in an iris-tinted light; saw little exquisite flecks of colour set here and there on the white expanse; watched all so intently, so wonderingly, that the numbness of her body became a throbbing pain before she was aware that she was enduring torture.

She strove to move, gave a little gasp; and he was down from his ladder and up on hers before her half-paralysed body had swayed to the edge of danger.

"Why didn't you say so?" he asked, sharply. "I can't keep track of time when I'm working!"

With arms and fingers that scarcely obeyed her she contrived to gather the white wool covering around her shoulders and limbs and lay back.

"You know," he said, "that it's foolish to act this way. I don't want to kill you, Miss West."

She only lowered her head amid its lovely crown of hair.

"You know your own limits," he said, resentfully. He looked down at the big clock: "It's a full hour. You had only to speak. Why didn't you?"

"I—I didn't know what to say."

"Didn't know!" He paused, astonished. Then: "Well, you felt yourself getting numb, didn't you?"

"Y-yes. But I thought it was—to be expected"— she blushed vividly under his astonished gaze: "I think I had better tell you that—that this is—the first time."

"The first time!"

"Yes. . . . I ought to have told you. I was afraid you might not want me."

17

"Lord above!" he breathed. "You poor—poor little thing!"

She began to cry silently; he saw the drops fall shining on the white wool robe, and leaned one elbow on the ladder, watching them. After a while they ceased, but she still held her head low, and her face was bent in the warm shadow of her hair.

"How could I understand?" he asked very gently.

"I—should have told you. I was afraid."

He said: "I'm terribly sorry. It must have been perfect torture for you to undress—to come into the studio. If you'd only given me an idea of how matters stood I could have made it a little easier. I'm afraid I was brusque—taking it for granted that you were a model and knew your business. . . . I'm terribly sorry."

She lifted her head, looked at him, with the tears still clinging to her lashes.

"You have been very nice to me. It is all my own fault."

He smiled. "Then it's all right, now that we understand. Isn't it?"

"Yes."

"You make a stunning model," he said frankly.

"Do I? Then you will let me come again?"

"*Let* you!" He laughed; "I'll be more likely to beg you."

"Oh, you won't have to," she said; "I'll come as long as you want me."

"That is simply angelic of you. Tell me, do you wish to descend to terra firma?"

She glanced below, doubtfully:

"N-no, thank you. If I could only stretch my—legs——"

" Stretch away," he said, much amused, " but don't tumble off and break into pieces. I like you better as you are than as an antique and limbless Venus."

She cautiously and daintily extended first one leg then the other under the wool robe, then eased the cramped muscles of her back, straightening her body and flexing her arms with a little sigh of relief. As her shy sidelong gaze reverted to him she saw to her relief that he was not noticing her. A slight sense of warmth suffused her body, and she stretched herself again, more confidently, and ventured to glance around.

" Speaking of terms," he said in an absent way, apparently preoccupied with the palette which he was carefully scraping, " do you happen to know what is the usual recompense for a model's service? "

She said that she had heard, and added with quick diffidence that she could not expect so much, being only a beginner.

He polished the surface of the palette with a handful of cheese cloth:

" Don't you think that you are worth it? "

" How can I be until I know how to pose for you? "

" You will never have to learn how to pose, Miss West."

" I don't know exactly what you mean."

" I mean that some models never learn. Some know how already—you, for example."

She flushed slightly: " Do you really mean that? "

" Oh, I wouldn't say so if I didn't. It's merely necessary for you to accustom yourself to holding a pose; the rest you already know instinctively."

" What is the rest? " she ventured to ask. " I don't quite understand what you see in me——"

"Well," he said placidly, "you are beautifully made. That is nine-tenths of the matter. Your head is set logically on your neck, and your neck is correctly placed on your spine, and your legs and arms are properly attached to your torso—your entire body, anatomically speaking, is hinged, hung, supported, developed as the ideal body should be. It's undeformed, unmarred, unspoiled, and that's partly luck, partly inheritance, and mostly decent habits and digestion."

She was listening intently, interested, surprised, her pink lips slightly parted.

"Another point," he continued; "you seem unable to move or rest ungracefully. Few women are so built that an ungraceful motion is impossible for them. You are one of the few. It's all a matter of anatomy."

She remained silent, watching him curiously.

He said: "But the final clincher to your qualifications is that you are intelligent. I have known pretty women," he added with sarcasm, "who were not what learned men would call precisely intelligent. But you are. I showed you my sketch, indicated in a general way what I wanted, and instinctively and intelligently you assumed the proper attitude. I didn't have to take you by the chin and twist your head as though you were a lay figure; I didn't have to pull you about and flex and bend and twist you. You knew that I wanted you to look like some sort of an ethereal immortality, deliciously relaxed, adrift in sunset clouds. And you *were* it—somehow or other."

She looked down, thoughtfully, nestling to the chin in the white wool folds. A smile, almost imperceptible, curved her lips.

"You are making it very easy for me," she said.

"You make it easy for yourself."

"I was horribly afraid," she said thoughtfully.

"I have no doubt of it."

"Oh, you don't know—nobody can know—no man can understand the terror of—of the first time——"

"It must be a ghastly experience."

"It is!—I don't mean that you have not done everything to make it easier—but—there in the little room—my courage left me—I almost died. I'd have run away only—I was afraid you wouldn't let me——"

He began to laugh; she tried to, but the terror of it all was as yet too recent.

"At first," she said, "I was afraid I wouldn't do for a model—not exactly afraid of my—my appearance, but because I was a novice; and I imagined that one had to know exactly how to pose——"

"I think," he interrupted smilingly, "that you might take the pose again if you are rested. Go on talking; I don't mind it."

She sat erect, loosened the white wool robe and dropped it from her with less consciousness and effort than before. Very carefully she set her feet on the blocks, fitting the shapely heels to the chalked outlines; found the mark for her elbow, adjusted her slim, smooth body and looked at him, flushing.

"All right," he said briefly; " go ahead and talk to me."

"Do you wish me to? "

"Yes; I'd rather."

"I don't know exactly what to say."

"Say anything," he returned absently, selecting a flat brush with a very long handle.

She thought a moment, then, lifting her eyes:

"I might ask you your name."

"What? Don't you know it? Oh, Lord! Oh, Vanity! I thought you'd heard of me."

She blushed, confused by her ignorance and what she feared was annoyance on his part; then perceived that he was merely amused; and her face cleared.

"We folk who create concrete amusement for the public always imagine ourselves much better known to that public than we are, Miss West. It's our little vanity—rather harmless after all. We're a pretty decent lot, sometimes absurd, especially in our tragic moments; sometimes emotional, usually illogical, often impulsive, frequently tender-hearted as well as super-sensitive.

"Now it was a pleasant little vanity for me to take it for granted that somehow you had heard of me and had climbed twelve flights of stairs for the privilege of sitting for me."

He laughed so frankly that the shy, responsive smile made her face enchanting; and he coolly took advantage of it, and while exciting and stimulating it, affixed it immortally on the exquisite creature he was painting.

"So you didn't climb those twelve flights solely for the privilege of having me paint you?"

"No," she admitted, laughingly, "I was merely going to begin at the top and apply for work all the way down until somebody took me—or nobody took me."

"But why begin at the top?"

"It is easier to bear disappointment going down," she said, seriously; "if two or three artists had refused me on the first and second floors, my legs would not have carried me up very far."

22

"Bad logic," he commented. "We mount by experience, using our wrecked hopes as footholds."

"You don't know how much a girl can endure. There comes a time—after years of steady descent—when misfortune and disappointment become endurable; when hope deferred no longer sickens. It is in rising toward better things that disappointments hurt most cruelly."

He turned his head in surprise; then went on painting:

"Your philosophy is the philosophy of submission."

"Do you call a struggle of years, submission?"

"But it was giving up after all—acquiescence, despondency, a *laissez faire* policy."

"One may tire of fighting."

"One may. Another may not."

"I think you have never had to fight very hard."

He turned his head abruptly; after a moment's silent survey of her, he resumed his painting with a sharp, impersonal glance before every swift and decisive brush stroke:

"No; I have never had to fight, Miss West. . . . It was keen of you to recognise it. I have never had to fight at all. Things come easily to me—things have a habit of coming my way. . . . I suppose I'm not exactly the man to lecture anybody on the art of fighting fortune. She's always been decent to me. . . . Sometimes I'm afraid—I have an instinct that she's too friendly. . . . And it troubles me. Do you understand what I mean?"

"Yes."

He looked up at her: "Are you sure?"

"I think so. I have been watching you painting.

23

I never imagined anybody could draw so swiftly, so easily—paint so surely, so accurately—that every brush stroke could be so—so significant, so decisive. . . . Is it not unusual? And is not that what is called facility?"

"Lord in Heaven!" he said; "what kind of a girl am I dealing with?—or what kind of a girl is dealing so unmercifully with me?"

"I—I didn't mean——"

"Yes, you did. Those very lovely and wonderfully shaped eyes of yours are not entirely for ornament. Inside that pretty head there's an apparatus designed for thinking; and it isn't idle."

He laughed gaily, a trifle defiantly:

"You've said it. You've found the fly in the amber. I'm cursed with facility. Worse still it gives me keenest pleasure to employ it. It does scare me occasionally—has for years—makes me miserable at intervals—fills me full of all kinds of fears and doubts."

He turned toward her, standing on his ladder, the big palette curving up over his left shoulder, a wet brush extended in his right hand:

"What shall I do!" he exclaimed so earnestly that she sat up straight, startled, forgetting her pose. "Ought I to stifle the vigour, the energy, the restless desire that drives me to express myself—that will not tolerate the inertia of calculation and ponderous reflection? Ought I to check myself, consider, worry, entangle myself in psychologics, seek for subtleties where none exist — split hairs, relapse into introspective philosophy when my fingers itch for a lump of charcoal and every colour on my set palette yells at me to be about my business?"

24

He passed the flat tip of his wet brush through the mass of rags in his left hand with a graceful motion like one unsheathing a sword:

"I tell you I do the things which I do, as easily, as naturally, as happily as any fool of a dicky-bird does his infernal twittering on an April morning. God knows whether there's anything in my work or in his twitter; but neither he nor I are likely to improve our output by pondering and cogitation. . . . Please resume the pose."

She did so, her dark young eyes on him; and he continued painting and talking in his clear, rapid, decisive manner:

"My name is Louis Neville. They call me Kelly —my friends do," he added, laughing. "Have you ever seen any of my work?"

"Yes."

He laughed again: "That's more soothing. However, I suppose you saw that big canvas of mine for the ceiling of the Metropolitan Museum's new northwest wing. The entire town saw it."

"Yes, I saw it."

"Did you care for it?"

She had cared for it too intensely to give him any adequate answer. Never before had her sense of colour and form and beauty been so exquisitely satisfied by the painted magic of any living painter. So this was the man who had enveloped her, swayed her senses, whirled her upward into his ocean of limpid light! This was the man who had done that miracle before which, all day long, crowds of the sober, decent, unimaginative—the solid, essentials of the nation—had lingered fascinated! This was the man—across there on

25

From his ladder he pointed with his brush to the preliminary sketch that faced her, touching figure after figure:

" I'm going to draw them in, now," he said; " first this one. Can you catch the pose? It's going to be hard; I'll block up your heels, later; that's it! Stand up straight, stretch as though the next moment you were going to rise on tiptoe and float upward without an effort——"

He was working like lightning in long, beautiful, clean outline strokes, brushed here and there with shadow shapes and masses. And time flew at first, then went slowly, more slowly, until it dragged at her delicate body and set every nerve aching.

" I—may I rest a moment? "

" Sure thing! " he said, cordially, laying aside palette and brushes. " Come on, Miss West, and we'll have luncheon."

She hastily swathed herself in the wool robe.

" Do you mean—here? "

" Yes. There's a dumb-waiter. I'll ring for the card."

" I'd like to," she said, " but do you think I had better? "

" Why not? "

" You mean—take lunch with you? "

" Why not? "

" Is it customary? "

" No, it isn't."

" Then I think I will go out to lunch some-where——"

" I'm not going to let you get away," he said, laughing. " You're too good to be real; I'm worried

"I—don't—want to—" she began; but he went away into the hall, rang, and presently she heard the ascending clatter of a dumb-waiter. From it he took the luncheon card and returned to where she was sitting at a rococo table. She blushed as he laid the card before her, and would have nothing to do with it. The result was that he did the ordering, sent the dumb-waiter down with his scribbled memorandum, and came wandering back with long, cool glances at his canvas and the work he had done on it.

"I mean to make a stunning thing of it," he remarked, eying the huge chassis critically. "All this—deviltry—whatever it is inside of me—must come out somehow. And that canvas is the place for it." He laughed and sat down opposite her:

"Man is born to folly, Miss West—born full of it. I get rid of mine on canvas. It's a safer outlet for original sin than some other ways."

She lay back in her antique gilded chair, hands extended along the arms, looking at him with a smile that was still shy.

"My idea of you—of an artist—was so different," she said.

"There are all kinds, mostly the seriously inspired and humourless variety who makes a mystic religion of a very respectable profession. This world is full of pale, enraptured artists; full of muscular, thumb-smearing artists; full of dreamy weavers of visions, usually deficient in spinal process; full of unwashed little inverts to whom the world really resembles a kaleidoscope full of things that wiggle——"

They began to laugh, he with a singular delight in her comprehension of his idle, irresponsible chatter, she

29

" Posing? "

" Yes."

" I don't quite understand you."

" Why, I only mean that—the other "—she smiled—
" what you call the bow-wows, would not have been an
outlet for me. . . . I was a show-girl for two months
last winter; I ought to know. And I'd rather have
died than——"

" I see," he said; " that outlet was too stupid to
have attracted you."

She nodded. " Besides, I have principles," she
said, candidly.

" Which effectually blocked that outlet. They sometimes kill, too, as you say. Youth stifled too long means
death—the death of youth at least. Outlets mean life.
The idea is to find a safe one."

She flushed in quick, sensitive response:.

" *That* is it; that is what I meant. Mr. Neville, I am
twenty-one; and do you know I never had a childhood?
And I am simply wild for it—for the girlhood and the
playtime that I never had——"

She checked herself, looking across at him uncertainly.

" Go on," he nodded.

" That is all."

" No; tell me the rest."

She sat with head bent, slender fingers picking at
her napkin; then, without raising her troubled eyes:

" Life has been—curious. My mother was bedrid-
den. My childhood and girlhood were passed caring for
her. That is all I ever did until—a year ago," she
added; her voice falling so low he could scarcely hear
her.

" She died, then? "

" A year ago last February."

" You went to school. You must have made friends there."

" I went to a public school for a year. After that mother taught me."

" She must have been extremely cultivated."

The girl nodded, looking absently at the cloth. Then, glancing up:

" I wonder whether you will understand me when I tell you why I decided to ask employment of artists."

" I'll try to," he said, smiling.

" It was an intense desire to be among cultivated people—if only for a few hours. Besides, I had read about artists; and their lives seemed so young, so gay, so worth living—please don't think me foolish and immature, Mr. Neville—but I was so stifled, so cut off from such people, so uninspired, so—so starved for a little gaiety—and I needed youthful companionship—surroundings where people of my own age and intelligence sometimes entered—and I had never had it——"

She looked at him with a strained, wistful expression as though begging him to understand her:

" I couldn't remain at the theatre," she said. " I had little talent—no chance except chances I would not tolerate; no companionship except what I was unfitted for by education and inclination. . . . The men were —impossible. There may have been girls I could have liked—but I did not meet them. So, as I had to do something—and my years of seclusion with mother had unfitted me for any business—for office work or shop work—I thought that artists might care to employ me —might give me—or let me see—be near—something

34

CHAPTER II

SPRING came unusually early that year. By the
first of the month a few willows and thorn bushes in the
Park had turned green; then, in a single day, the entire
Park became lovely with golden bell-flowers, and the
first mowing machine clinked over the greenswards leaving a fragrance of clipped verdure in its wake.

Under a characteristic blue sky April unfolded its
myriad leaves beneath which robins ran over shaven
lawns and purple grackle bustled busily about, and
the water fowl quacked and whistled and rushed through
the water nipping and chasing one another or, sidling
alongside, began that nodding, bowing, bobbing acquaintance preliminary to aquatic courtship.

Many of the wild birds had mated; many were mat-
ing; amorous caterwauling on back fences made night
an inferno; pigeons cooed and bubbled and made endless
nuisances of themselves all day long.

In lofts, offices, and shops youthful faces, whitened
by the winter's pallour, appeared at open windows gazing into the blue above, or, with pretty, inscrutable
eyes, studied the passing throng till the lifted eyes of
youth below completed the occult circuit with a smile.

And the spring sunshine grew hot, and sprinkling
carts appeared, and the metropolis moulted its over-
coats, and the derby became a burden, and the annual

spring exhibition of the National Academy of Design remained uncrowded.

Neville, lunching at the Syrinx Club, carelessly caught the ball of conversation tossed toward him and contributed his final comment:

"Burleson — and you, Sam Ogilvy — and you, Annan, all say that the exhibition is rotten. You say so every year; so does the majority of people. And the majority will continue saying the same thing throughout the coming decades as long as there are any exhibitions to damn.

"It is the same thing in other countries. For a hundred years the majority has pronounced every Salon rotten. And it will so continue.

"But the facts are these: the average does not vary much. A mediocrity, not disagreeable, always rules; supremity has been, is, and always will be the stick in the riffle around which the little whirlpool will always centre. This year it happens to be José Querida who stems the sparkling mediocrity and sticks up from the bottom gravel making a fine little swirl. Next year —or next decade it may be anybody—you, Annan, or Sam—perhaps," he added with a slight smile, "it might be I. *Quand même*. The exhibitions are no rottener than they have ever been; and it's up to us to go about our business. And I'm going. Goodbye."

He rose from the table, laid aside the remains of his cigar, nodded good-humouredly to the others, and went out with that quick, graceful, elastic step which was noticed by everybody and envied by many.

"Hell," observed John Burleson, hitching his broad shoulders forward and swallowing a goblet of claret

" There is—there always has been something lacking in all that big, glorious, splendid work. It only needs that one thing—whatever it is," said Ogilvy, quietly. " Kelly is too sure, too powerfully perfect, too omniscient——"

" And we mortals can't stand that," commented Annan, laughing. " 'Raus mit Neville!' He paints joy and sorrow as though he'd never known either——"

And his voice checked itself of its own instinct in the startled silence.

" That man, Neville, has never known the pain of work," said Gail, deliberately. " When he has passed through it and it has made his hand less steady, less omnipotent——"

" That's right. We can't love a man who has never endured what we have," said another. " No genius can hide his own immunity. That man paints with an unscarred soul. A little hell for his—and no living painter could stand beside him."

" Piffle," observed John Burleson.

Ogilvy said: " It is true, I think, that out of human suffering a quality is distilled which affects everything one does. Those who have known sorrow can best depict it—not perhaps most plausibly, but most convincingly—and with fewer accessories, more reticence, and—better taste."

" Why do you want to paint tragedies? " demanded Burleson.

" One need not paint them, John, but one needs to understand them to paint anything else—needs to have lived them, perhaps, to become a master of pictured happiness, physical or spiritual."

" She's a dream," said Ogilvy—" *un peu sauvage* —no inclination to socialism there, Annan. I know because I was considering the advisability of bestowing upon her one of those innocent, inadvertent, and fascinatingly chaste salutes—just to break the formality. She wouldn't have it. I'd taken her to the theatre, too. Girls are astonishing problems."

" You're a joyous beast, aren't you, Sam? " observed Burleson.

" I may be a trifle joyous. I tried to explain that to her, but she wouldn't listen. Heaven knows my intentions are child-like. I liked her because she's the sort of girl you can take anywhere and not queer yourself if you collide with your fiancée—visiting relative from 'Frisco, you know. She's equipped to impersonate anything from the younger set to the prune and pickle class."

" She certainly is a looker," nodded Annan.

" She can deliver the cultivated goods, too, and make a perfectly good play at the unsophisticated intellectual," said Ogilvy with conviction. " And it's a rare combination to find a dream that looks as real at the Opera as it does in a lobster palace. But she's no socialist, Harry—she'll ride in a taxi with you and sit up half the night with you, but it's nix for getting closer, and the frozen Fownes for the chaste embrace— that's all."

" She's a curious kind of girl," mused Burleson ;— " seems perfectly willing to go about with you ;—enjoys it like one of those bread-and-butter objects that the department shops call a ' Miss.' "

Annan said: " The girl is unusual, everyway. You don't know where to place her. She's a girl without a caste. I like her. I made some studies from her; Kelly let me."

" Does Kelly own her? " asked Burleson, puffing out his chest.

" He discovered her. He has first call."

Allaire, who had come up, caught the drift of the conversation.

" Oh, hell," he said, in his loud, careless voice, " anybody can take Valerie West to supper. The town's full of her kind."

" Have you taken her anywhere? " asked Annan, casually.

Allaire flushed up: " I haven't had time." He added something which changed the fixed smile on his symmetrical, highly coloured face into an expression not entirely agreeable.

" The girl's all right," said Burleson, reddening. " She's damn decent to everybody. What are you talking about, Allaire? Kelly will put a head on you! "

Allaire, careless and assertive, shrugged away the rebuke with a laugh:

" Neville is one of those professional virgins we read about in our neatly manicured fiction. He's what is known as the original mark. Jezebel and Potiphar's wife in combination with Salome and the daughters of Lot couldn't disturb his confidence in them or in himself. And—in my opinion—he paints that way, too." And he went away laughing and swinging his athletic shoulders and twirling his cane, his hat not mathematically straight on his handsome, curly head.

" There strides a joyous bounder," observed Ogilvy.

" Curious," mused Annan. " His family is oldest New York. You see 'em that way, at times."

"Your composition is one magnificent vista of legs, Kelly," insisted Ogilvy. "Put pants on those swans."

Neville merely turned and threw an empty paint tube at him, and continued his cloud outlining with undisturbed composure.

"Where have you been, Rita?" asked Ogilvy, dropping into a chair. "Nobody sees you any more."

"That's because nobody went to the show, and that's why they took it off," said Rita Tevis, resentfully. "I had a perfectly good part which nobody crabbed because nobody wanted it, which suited me beautifully because I hate to have anything that others want. Now there's nothing doing in the millinery line and I'm ready for suggestions."

"Dinner with me," said Ogilvy, fondly. But she turned up her dainty nose:

"Have *you* anything more interesting to offer, Mr. Annan?"

"Only my heart, hand, and Ogilvy's fortune," said Annan, regretfully. "But I believe Archie Allaire was looking for a model of your type——"

"I don't want to pose for Mr. Allaire," said the girl, pouting and twirling the handle of her parasol.

But neither Annan nor Ogilvy could use her then; and Neville had just finished a solid week of her.

"What I'll do," she said with decision, "will be to telephone John Burleson. I never knew him to fail a girl in search of an engagement."

"Isn't he a dear," said Valerie, smiling. "I adore him."

She sat at the piano, running her fingers lightly over the keyboard, listening to what was being said, watching with happy interest everything that was going on around her, and casting an occasional glance over her shoulder and upward to where Neville stood at work.

"John Burleson," observed Rita, looking fixedly at Ogilvy, " is easily the nicest man I know."

"Help!" said Ogilvy, feebly.

Valerie glanced across the top of the piano, laughing, while her hands passed idly here and there over the keys:

"Sam *can* be very nice, Rita; but you've got to make him," she said.

"Did you ever know a really interesting man who didn't require watching?" inquired Annan, mildly.

Rita surveyed him with disdain: "Plenty."

"Don't believe it. No girl has any very enthusiastic use for a man in whom she has perfect confidence."

"Here's another profound observation," added Ogilvy; "when a woman loses confidence in a man she finds a brand-new interest in him. But when a man once really loses confidence in a woman, he never regains it, and it's the beginning of the end. What do you think about that, Miss West?"

Valerie, still smiling, struck a light chord or two, considering:

"I don't know how it would be," she said, "to lose confidence in a man you really care much about. I should think it would break a girl's heart."

"It doesn't," said Rita, with supreme contempt. "You become accustomed to it."

Valerie leaned forward against the keyboard, laughing:

"Oh, Rita!" she said, "what a confession!"

"You silly child," retorted Rita, "I'm twenty-two.

"Art's a bum mistress if she makes you hustle like that!" commented Ogilvy. "Shake her, Kelly. She's a wampire mit a sarpint's tongue!"

"The worst of Kelly is that he'd *rather* paint," said Annan, hopelessly. "It's sufficient to sicken the proverbial cat."

"Get a machine and take us all out to Woodmanston?" suggested Ogilvy. "It's a bee—u—tiful day, dearie!"

"Get out of here!" retorted Neville, painting composedly.

"Your industry saddens us," insisted Annan. "It's only in mediocrity that you encounter industry. Genius frivols; talent takes numerous vacations on itself——"

"And at its own expense," added Valerie, demurely. "I knew a man who couldn't finish his 'Spring Academy' in time: and he had all winter to finish it. But he didn't. Did you ever hear about that man, Sam?"

"Me," said Ogilvy, bowing with hand on heart. "And with that cruel jab from *you*—false fair one— I'll continue heavenward in the elevator. Come on, Harry."

Annan took an elaborate farewell of Valerie which she met in the same mock-serious manner; then she waved a gay and dainty adieu to Ogilvy, and reseated herself after their departure. But this time she settled down into a great armchair facing Neville and his canvas, and lay back extending her arms and resting the back of her head on the cushions.

Whether or not Neville was conscious of her presence below she could not determine, so preoccupied did he appear to be with the work in hand. She lay there in the pleasant, mellow light of the great windows, watching him, at first intently, then, soothed by the soft spring wind that fitfully stirred the hair at her temples, she relaxed her attention, idly contented, happy without any particular reason.

Now and then a pigeon flashed by the windows, sheering away high above the sunlit city. Once, wind-caught, or wandering into unaccustomed heights, high in the blue a white butterfly glimmered, still mounting to infinite altitudes, fluttering, breeze-blown, a silvery speck adrift.

"Like a poor soul aspiring," she thought listlessly, watching with dark eyes over which the lids dropped lazily at moments, only to lift again as her gaze reverted to the man above.

She thought about him, too; she usually did—about his niceness to her, his never-to-be-forgotten kindness; her own gratitude to him for her never-to-be-forgotten initiation.

It seemed scarcely possible that two months had passed since her novitiate—that two months ago she still knew nothing of the people, the friendships, the interest, the surcease from loneliness and hopeless apathy, that these new conditions had brought to her.

Had she known Louis Neville only two months? Did all this new buoyancy date from two short months' experience—this quickened interest in life, this happy development of intelligence so long starved, this unfolding of youth in the atmosphere of youth? She found it difficult to realise, lying there so contentedly, so happily, following, with an interest and appreciation always developing, the progress of the work.

Already, to herself, she could interpret much that she saw in this new world. Cant phrases, bits of studio

She was thinking of this, now, as she lay there watching him.

He had added: "Enthusiasm is excellent while you're dressing for breakfast; but good pictures are painted in cold blood. Go out into the back yard and yell your appreciation of the universe if you want to; but the studio is a silent place; and a blank canvas a mathematical proposition."

Could this be true? Was all the beauty, all the joyous charm, all the splendour of shape and colour the result of working out a mathematical proposition? Was this exquisite surety of touch and handling, of mass and line composition, all these lovely depths and vast ethereal spaces superbly peopled, merely the logical result of solving that problem? Was it all clear, limpid, steady, nerveless intelligence; and was nothing due to the chance and hazard of inspiration?

Gladys, the cat, walked in, gently flourishing her tail, hesitated, looked around with narrowing green-jewelled eyes, and, ignoring the whispered invitation and the outstretched hand, leaped lightly to a chair and settled down on a silken cushion, paws and tail folded under her jet-black body.

Valerie reproached her in a whisper, reminding her of past caresses and attentions, but the cat only blinked at her pleasantly.

On a low revolving stand at Valerie's elbow lay a large lump of green modelling wax. This wax Neville sometimes used to fashion, with his facile hands, little figures sketched from his models. These he arranged in groups as though to verify the composition on the canvas before him, and this work and the pliant material which he employed had for her a particular and never-a perfectly heavenly degree what to you and others may be commonplace and uninteresting? All I ask is to be permitted to enjoy it while I am still young enough. I—I *must!* I really need it, Mr. Neville. It seems, at moments, as if I could never have enough—after the years—where I had—nothing."

Neville had begun walking to and fro in front of her with the quick, decisive step that characterised his movements; but his restlessness seemed only to emphasise the attention he concentrated on every word she spoke; and, though he merely glanced at her from moment to moment, she was conscious that the man now understood, and was responding more directly to her than ever before in their brief and superficial acquaintance.

"I don't want to go away and study," she said. "It is perfectly dear of you to offer it—I—there is no use in trying to thank you——"

"Valerie!"

"What!" she said, startled by his use of her given name for the first time in their acquaintance.

He said, smilingly grave: "You didn't think there was a string attached to anything I offered?"

"A—a string?"

"Did you?"

She blushed hotly: "No, of course not."

"It's all right then," he nodded; but she began to think of that new idea in a confused, startled, helpless sort of way.

"How could you think *that* of me?" she faltered.

"I didn't——"

"You—it must have been in your mind——"

"I wanted to be sure it wasn't in *yours*——"

"You ought to have known! Haven't you learned anything at all about me in two months?"

"Do you think any man can learn anything about anybody in two months?" he asked, lightly.

"Yes, I do. I've learned a good deal about you—enough, anyway, not to attribute anything—unworthy——"

"You silly child; you've learned nothing about me if that's what you think you've discovered."

"I *have* discovered it!" she retorted, tremulously; "I've learned horrid things about other men, too—and they're not like you!"

"Valerie! Valerie! I'm precisely like all the rest—my selfishness is a little more concentrated than theirs, that's the only difference. For God's sake don't make a god of me."

She sat down on the head of the sofa, looking straight at him, pretty head lowered a trifle so that her gaze was accented by the lovely level of her brows:

"I've long wanted to have a thorough talk with you," she said. "Have you got time now?"

He hesitated, controlling his secret amusement under an anxious gravity as he consulted the clock.

"Suppose you give me an hour on those figures up there? The light will be too poor to work by in another hour. Then we'll have tea and 'thorough talks.'"

"All right," she said, calmly.

He picked up palette and mahl-stick and mounted to his perch on the scaffolding; she walked slowly into the farther room, stood motionless a moment, then raising both arms she began to unhook the collar of her gown.

When she was ready she stepped into her sandals,

and great are too nearly extinct for such familiarity. Call me *Mr.* Kelly."

"I won't. You are only a big boy, anyway—Louis Neville—and sometimes I shall call you Kelly, and sometimes Louis, and very occasionally Mr. Neville."

"All right," he said, absently—"only hold that distractingly ornamental head and those incomparable shoulders a trifle more steady, please—rest solidly on the left leg—let the right hip fall into its natural position—*that's* it. Thank you."

Holding the pose her eyes wandered from him and his canvas to the evening tinted clouds already edged with deeper gold. Through the sheet of glass above she saw a shred of white fleece in mid-heaven turn to a pale pink.

"I wonder why you asked me to tea?" she mused.

"What?" He turned around to look at her.

"You never before asked me to do such a thing," she said, candidly. "You're an absent-minded man, Mr. Neville."

"It never occurred to me," he retorted, amused. "Tea is weak-minded."

"It occurred to me. That's what part of my 'thorough talk' is to be about; your carelessness in noticing me except professionally."

He continued working, rapidly now; and it seemed to her as though something—a hint of the sombre—had come into his face—nothing definite—but the smile was no longer there, and the brows were slightly knitted.

Later he glanced up impatiently at the sky: the summer clouds wore a deeper rose and gold.

"We'd better have our foolish tea," he said, abruptly, driving his brushes into a bowl of black soap

70

and laying aside his palette for his servant to clean later.

For a while, not noticing her, he fussed about his canvas, using a knife here, a rag there, passing to and fro across the scaffolding, oblivious of the flight of time, until at length the waning light began to prophesy dusk, and he came to himself with a guilty start.

Below, in the studio, Valerie sat, fully dressed except for hat and gloves, head resting in the padded depths of an armchair, watching him in silence.

"I declare," he said, looking down at her contritely, "I never meant to keep you all this time. Good Lord! Have I been puttering up here for an hour and a half! It's nearly eight o'clock! Why on earth didn't you speak to me, Valerie?"

"It's a braver girl than I am who'll venture to interrupt you at work, Kelly," she said, laughingly. "I'm a little afraid of you."

"Nonsense! I wasn't doing anything. My Heaven! —can it be eight o'clock?"

"It is. . . . You *said* we were going to have tea."

"Tea! Child, you can't have tea at eight o'clock! I'm terribly sorry"—he came down the ladder, vexed with himself, wiping the paint from his hands with a bunch of cheese cloth—"I'm humiliated and ashamed, Miss West. Wait a moment——"

He walked hastily through the next room into his small suite of apartments, washed his hands, changed his painter's linen blouse for his street coat, and came back into the dim studio.

"I'm really sorry, Valerie," he said. "It was rotten rude of me."

"So am I sorry. It's absurd, but I feel like a per-

citement of taking a cup of weak tea with me," he said,
jestingly—"after all those jolly dinners and suppers
and theatres and motor parties that I hear about?"

She nodded and held out her hand with decision:
"Good-night."

He retained her hand a moment, not meaning to—
not really intending to ask her what he did ask her.
And she raised her velvet eyes gravely:

"Do you really want me?"

"Yes. . . . I don't know why I never asked you before——"

"It was absurd not to," she said, impulsively; "I'd
have gone anywhere with you the first day I ever knew
you! Besides, I dress well enough for you not to be
ashamed of me."

He began to laugh: "Valerie, you funny little
thing! You funny, funny little thing!"

"Not in the slightest," she retorted, sedately. "I'm
having a heavenly time for the first time in my life, and
I have so wanted you to be part of it . . . of course
you *are* part of it," she added, hastily—"most of it! I
only meant that I—I'd like to be a little in your other
life—have you enter mine, a little—just so I can remember, in years to come, an evening with you now and
then—to see things going on around us—to hear what
you think of things that we see together. . . . Because,
with you, I feel so divinely free, so unembarrassed, so
entirely off my guard. . . . I don't mean to say that I
don't have a splendid time with the others even when I
have to watch them; I do—and even the watching is
fun——"

The child-like audacity and laughing frankness, the
confidence of her attitude toward him were delightfully

refreshing. He looked into her pretty, eager, engaging face, smiling, captivated.

"Valerie," he said, "tell me something—will you?"

"Yes, if I can."

"I'm more or less of a painting machine. I've made myself so, deliberately—to the exclusion of other interests. I wonder"—he looked at her musingly—"whether I'm carrying it too far for my own good."

"I don't understand."

"I mean—is there anything machine-made about my work? Does it lack—does it lack anything?"

"No!" she said, indignantly loyal. "Why do you ask me that?"

"People—some people say it does lack—a certain quality."

She said with supreme contempt: "You must not believe them. I also hear things—and I know it is an unworthy jealousy that——"

"What have you heard?" he interrupted.

"Absurdities. I don't wish even to think of them——"

"I wish you to. Please. Such things are sometimes significant."

"But—is there any significance in what a few envious artists say—or a few silly models——"

"More significance in what they say than in a whole chorus of professional critics."

"Are you serious?" she asked, astonished.

"Perfectly. Without naming anybody or betraying any confidence, what have you heard in criticism of my work? It's from models and brother painters that the real truth comes—usually distorted, half told, maliciously hinted sometimes—but usually the germ of truth

"Have you never cared, very much, for anybody—any woman?"

"Not sentimentally," he returned, laughing. "Do you think that a good course of modern flirtation—a thorough schooling in the old-fashioned misfortunes of true love would inject into my canvases that elusively occult quality they're all howling for?"

She remained smilingly silent.

"Perhaps something less strenuous would do," he said, mischievously—"a pretty amourette?—just one of those gay, frivolous, Louis XV affairs with some daintily receptive girl, not really improper, but only ultra fashionable. Do you think *that* would help some, Valerie?"

She raised her eyes, still smiling, a little incredulous, very slightly embarrassed:

"I don't think your painting requires any such sacrifices of you, Mr. Neville. . . . Are you going to take me somewhere to dinner? I'm dreadfully hungry."

"You poor little girl, of course I am. Besides, you must be suffering under the terrible suppression of that 'thorough talk' which you——"

"It doesn't really require a thorough talk," she said; "I'll tell you now what I had to say. No, don't interrupt, please! I want to—please let me—so that nothing will mar our enjoyment of each other and of the gay world around us when we are dining. . . . It is this: Sometimes—once in a while—I become absurdly lonely, which makes me a fool, temporarily. And—will you let me telephone you at such times?—just to talk to you—perhaps see you for a minute?"

"Of course. You know my telephone number. Call me up whenever you like."

"*Could* I see you at such moments? I—there's a—some—a kind of sentiment about me—when I'm *very* lonely; and I've been foolish enough to let one or two men see it—in fact I've been rather indiscreet—silly—with a man—several men—now and then. A lonely girl is easily sympathised with—and rather likes it; and is inclined to let herself go a little. . . . I don't want to. . . . And at times I've done it. . . . Sam Ogilvy nearly kissed me, which really doesn't count—does it? But I let Harry Annan do it, once. . . . If I'm weak enough to drift into such silliness I'd better find a safeguard. I've been thinking—thinking—that it really does originate in a sort of foolish loneliness . . . not in anything worse. So I thought I'd have a thorough talk with you about it. I'm twenty-one—with all my experience of life and of men crowded into a single winter and spring. I have as friends only the few people I have met through you. I have nobody to see unless I see them—nowhere to go unless I go where they ask me. . . . So I thought I'd ask you to let me depend a little on you, sometimes—as a refuge from isolation and morbid thinking now and then. And from other mischief—for which I apparently have a capacity—to judge by what I've done—and what I've let men do already."

She laid her hand lightly on his arm in sudden and impulsive confidence:

"That's my 'thorough talk.' I haven't any one else to tell it to. And I've told you the worst." She smiled at him adorably: "And now I am ready to go out with you," she said,—" go anywhere in the world with you, Kelly. And I am going to be perfectly happy —if you are."

"Rita! You *said* you enjoyed that excursion!" exclaimed Ogilvy, with pathos.

"I said it to flatter that enormous vanity of yours, Sam. I had a perfectly wretched time."

"What sort of a time did you have last evening?" inquired Neville, turning from the picture.

"Horrid. Everybody ate too much, and Valerie spooned with a new man—I don't remember his name. She went out in a canoe with him and they sang 'She kissed him on the gangplank when the boat moved out.'"

Neville, silent, turned to the picture once more. In a low rapid voice he indicated to Ogilvy where matters might be differently treated, stepped back a few paces, nodded decisively, and turned again to Rita:

"I've been waiting for Miss West," he said. "Have you any reason to think that she might not keep her appointment this morning?"

"She had a headache when we got home," said Rita. "She stayed with me last night. I left her asleep. Why don't you ring her up. You know my number."

"All right," said Neville, shortly, and went out.

When he first tried to ring her up the wire was busy. It was a party wire, yet a curious uneasiness set him pacing the studio, smoking, brows knitted, until he decided it was time to try again.

This time he recognised her distant voice: "Hello—hello! *Is* that you, Mr. Neville?"

"Valerie!"

"Oh, it *is* you, Kelly? I hoped you would call me up. I *knew* it must be *you!*"

"Yes, it is. What the deuce is the matter? Are you ill?"

"Oh, dear, no!"

"*What*, then?"

"When he first tried to ring her up the wire was busy."

"I was *so* sleepy, Kelly. Please forgive me. We had such a late party—and it was daylight before I went to bed. Please forgive me; won't you?"

"When I called you a few minutes ago your wire was busy. Were you conversing?"

" Yes. I was talking to José Querida."

" H'm ! "

" José was with us last evening. . . . I went canoe-
ing with him. He just called me up to ask how I
felt."

" Hunh ! "

" What ? "

" Nothing."

" Are you annoyed, Louis? "

" No ! "

" Oh, I thought it sounded as though you were
irritated. I am so ashamed at having overslept. Who
told you I was here? Oh, Rita, I suppose. Poor child,
she was more faithful than I. The alarm clock woke
her and she was plucky enough to get up—and I
only yawned and thought of you, and I was *so* sleepy!
Are you sure you do forgive me? "

" Of course."

" You don't say it very kindly."

" I mean it cordially," he snapped. He could hear
her sigh: " I suppose you do." Then she added:

" I am dressing, Kelly. I don't wish for any breakfast, and I'll come to the studio as soon as I can——"

" Take your breakfast first ! "

" No, I really don't care for——"

" All right. Come ahead."

" I will. Good-bye, Kelly, dear."

He rang off, picked up the telephone again, called
the great Hotel Regina, and ordered breakfast sent to
his studio immediately.

When Valerie arrived she found silver, crystal, and
snowy linen awaiting her with chilled grapefruit,

African melon, fragrant coffee, toast, and pigeon's eggs poached on Astrakan caviar.

"Oh, Louis!" she exclaimed, enraptured; "I don't deserve this—but it is perfectly dear of you—and I *am* hungry! . . . Good-morning," she added, shyly extending a fresh cool hand; "I am really none the worse for wear you see."

That was plain enough. In her fresh and youthful beauty the only sign of the night's unwisdom was in the scarcely perceptible violet tint under her thick lashes. Her skin was clear and white and dewy fresh, her dark eyes unwearied—her gracefully slender presence fairly fragrant with health and vigour.

She seated herself—offered to share with him in dumb appeal, urged him in delicious pantomime, and smiled encouragingly as he reluctantly found a chair beside her and divided the magnificent melon.

"Did you have a good time?" he asked, trying not to speak ungraciously.

"Y-yes. . . . It was a silly sort of a time."

"Silly?"

"I was rather sentimental—with Querida."

He said nothing—grimly.

"I told you last night, Louis. Why couldn't you see me?"

"I was dining out; I couldn't."

She sipped her chilled grapefruit meditatively:

"I hadn't seen you for a week," she laughed, glancing sideways at him, "and that lonely feeling began about five o'clock; and I called you up at seven because I couldn't stand it. . . . But you wouldn't see me; and so when Rita and the others came in a big touring car —do you blame me very much for going with them?"

4

The imagery struck her as humorous and she laughed.

" Poor Kelly," she said aloud to herself, " he is used and abused and imposed upon, and in revenge he offers his ungrateful tormentor delicious breakfasts. *What* shall his reward be?——or must he await it in Paradise where he truly belongs amid the martyrs and the blessed saints!"

Neville grunted.

" Oh, *oh!* such a post-Raphaelite scowl! Job won't bow to you when you go aloft, Kelly. Besides, polite martyrs smile pleasantly while enduring torment. . . . What are you going to do with me to-day?" she added, glancing around with frank curiosity at an easel which was set with a full-length virgin canvas.

" Portrait," he replied, tersely.

" Oh," she said, surprised. He had never before painted her clothed.

From moment to moment, as she leisurely break-fasted, she glanced around at the canvas, interested in the new idea of his painting her draped; a trifle per-plexed, too.

" Louis," she said, " I don't quite see how you're ever going to find a purchaser for just a plain portrait of me."

He said, irritably: " I don't have to work for a liv-ing *every* minute, do I? For Heaven's sake give me a day off to study."

" But—it seems like wasted time——"

" What is wasted time?"

" Why just to paint a portrait of me as I am. Isn't it?" She looked up smilingly, perfectly innocent of any self-consciousness. " In the big canvases for the

88

Byzantine Theatre you always made my features too radiant, too glorious for portraits. It seems rather a slump to paint me as I am—just a girl in street clothes."

A singular expression passed over his face.

"Yes," he said, after a moment—"just a girl in street clothes. No clouds, no sky, no diaphanous draperies of silk; no folds of cloth of gold; no gemmed girdles, no jewels. Nothing of the old glamour, the old glory; no sunburst laced with mist; no 'light that never was on sea or land.' . . . Just a young girl standing in the half light of my studio. . . . And by God!—if I can not do it—the rest is worthless."

Amazed at his tone and expression she turned quickly, set back her cup, remained gazing at him, bewildered by the first note of bitterness she had ever heard in his voice.

He had risen and walked to his easel, back partly turned. She saw him fussing with his palette, colours, and brushes, watched him for a few moments, then she went away into the farther room where she had a glass shelf to herself with toilet requisites—a casual and dainty gift from him.

When she returned he was still bending over his colour-table; and she walked up and laid her hand on his shoulder—not quite understanding why she did it.

He straightened up to his full stature, surprised, turning his head to meet a very clear, very sweetly disturbed gaze.

"Kelly, dear, are you unhappy?"

"Why—no."

"You seem to be a little discontented.

Under her light hand she felt the impatient movement of his shoulders, and her hand fell away.

" Don't you care for it, now that it's finished? " she asked, wondering.

" I'm devilish sick of it," he said, so savagely that every nerve in her recoiled with a tiny shock. She remained silent, motionless, awaiting his pleasure. He set his palette, frowning. She had never before seen him like this.

After a while she said, quietly: " If you are waiting for me, please tell me what you expect me to do, because I don't know, Kelly."

" Oh, just stand over there," he said, vaguely; " just walk about and stop anywhere when you feel like stopping."

She walked a few steps at hazard, partly turned to look back at him with a movement adorable in its hesitation.

" Don't budge! " he said, brusquely.

" Am I to remain like this? "

" Exactly."

He picked up a bit of white chalk, went over to her, knelt down, and traced on the floor the outline of her shoes.

Then he went back, and, with his superbly cool assurance, began to draw with his brush upon the untouched canvas.

From where she stood, and as far as she could determine, he seemed, however, to work less rapidly than usual—with a trifle less decision—less precision. Another thing she noticed; the calm had vanished from his face. The vivid animation, the cool self-confidence, the half indolent relapse into careless certainty—all familiar phases of the man as she had so often seen him painting—were now not perceptible. There seemed to be, too, a curious lack of authority about his brush strokes at intervals—moments of grave perplexity, indecision almost resembling the hesitation of inexperience —and for the first time she saw in his gray eyes the narrowing concentration of mental uncertainty.

It seemed to her sometimes as though she were looking at a total stranger. She had never thought of him as having any capacity for the ordinary and lesser ills, vanities, and vexations—the trivial worries that beset other artists.

"Louis?" she said, full of curiosity.

"What?" he demanded, ungraciously.

"You are not one bit like yourself to-day."

He made no comment. She ventured again:

"Do I hold the pose properly?"

"Yes, thanks," he said, absently.

"May I talk?"

"I'd rather you didn't, Valerie, just at present."

"All right," she rejoined, cheerfully; but her pretty eyes watched him very earnestly, a little troubled.

When she was tired the pose ended; that had been their rule; but long after her neck and back and thighs and limbs begged for relief, she held the pose, reluctant to interrupt him. When at last she could endure it no longer she moved; but her right leg had lost not only all sense of feeling but all power to support her; and down she came with a surprised and frightened little exclamation—and he sprang to her and swung her to her feet again.

"Valerie! You bad little thing! Don't you know enough to stop when you're tired?"

earnest. " Suppose—suppose—" but she stopped suddenly, with a light little laugh that lingered pleasantly
in the vast, still room.

She said: " I begin to think that there are two Kellys
—no, *one* Kelly and *one* Louis. Kelly is familiar to
me; I seem to have known him all my life—the happy
part of my life. Louis I have just seen for the first
time—there at the easel, painting, peering from me to
his canvas with Kelly's good-looking eyes all narrow
with worry——"

" What on earth are you chattering about, Valerie? "

" You and Kelly. . . . I don't quite know which I
like best—the dear, sweet, kind, clever, brilliant, impersonal, god-like Kelly, or this new Louis—so very abrupt
in speaking to me——"

" Valerie, dear! Forgive me. I'm out of sorts somehow. It began—I don't know—waiting for you—wondering if you could be ill—all alone. Then that ass,
Sam Ogilvy—oh, it's just oversmoking I guess, or—I
don't know what."

She sat regarding him, head tipped unconsciously on
one side in an attitude suggesting a mind concocting
malice.

" Louis? "

" What? "

" You're very attractive when you're god-like——"

" You little wretch! "

" But—you're positively dangerous when you're
human."

" Valerie! I'll—— "

" The great god Kelly, or the fascinating, fearsome,
erring Louis! Which is it to be? I've an idea that the
time is come to decide! "

95

" Oh, Kelly, be lofty and Olympian! Be a god and shame the rest of us! "

" I'll shamefully resemble one of 'em in another moment if you continue tormenting me! "

" Which one, great one? "

" Jupiter, little lady. He was the boss philanderer you know."

" What is a philanderer, my Olympian friend? "

" Oh, one of those Olympian divinities who always began the day by kissing the girls all around."

" Before breakfast? "

" Certainly."

" It's—after breakfast, Kelly."

" Luncheon and dinner still impend."

" Besides—I'm not a bit lonely to-day. . . . I'm afraid I wouldn't let you, Kel—I mean Louis."

" Why didn't you say ' Kelly '? "

" Kelly is too god-like to kiss."

" Oh! So *that's* the difference! Kelly isn't human; Louis is."

" Kelly, to me," she admitted, " is practically kiss-less. . . . I haven't thought about Louis in that regard."

" Consider the matter thoroughly."

" Do you wish me to? " She bent her head, smiling. Then, looking up with enchanting audacity:

" I really don't know, Mr. Neville. Some day when I'm lonely—and if Louis is at home and Kelly is out—you and I might spend an evening together on a moon-lit lake and see how much of a human being Louis can be."

She laughed, watching him under the dark lashes, charming mouth mocking him in every curve.

" would you have the heart to destroy me after you've made me? "

" I don't know what I'd do, Valerie. I never felt just this way about anything. If I can't paint you—a human, breathing *you*—with all of you there on the canvas—*all* of you, soul, mind, and body—all of your beauty, your youth, your sadness, happiness—your errors, your nobility—*you*, Valerie!—then there's no telling what I'll do."

She said nothing. Presently she resumed the pose and he his painting.

It became very still in the sunny studio.

CHAPTER IV

In that month of June, for the first time in his deliberately active career, Neville experienced a disinclination to paint. And when he realised that it was disinclination, it appalled him. Something—he didn't understand what—had suddenly left him satiated—and with all the uneasiness and discontent of satiation he forced matters until he could force no further.

He had commissions, several, and valuable; and let them lie. For the first time in all his life the blank canvas of an unexecuted commission left him untempted, unresponsive, weary.

He had, also, his portrait of Valerie to continue. He continued it mentally, at intervals; but for several days, now, he had not laid a brush to it.

"It's funny," he said to Querida, going out on the train to his sister's country home one delicious morning—"it's confoundedly odd that I should turn lazy in my old age. Do you think I'm worked out?" He gulped down a sudden throb of fear smilingly.

"Lie fallow," said Querida, gently. "No soil is deep enough to yield without rest."

"Yours does."

"Oh, for me," said Querida, showing his snowy teeth, "I often sicken of my fat sunlight, frying everything to an iridescent omelette." He shrugged, laughed: "I turn lazy for months every year. Try it, my friend. Don't you even keep *mi-carême?*"

101

Neville stared out of the window at the station platform past which they were gliding, and rose with Querida as the train stopped. His sister's touring car was waiting; into it stepped Querida, and he followed; and away they sped over the beautiful rolling country, where handsome cattle tried to behave like genuine Troyon's, and silvery sheep attempted to imitate Mauve, and even the trees, separately or in groups, did their best to look like sections of Rousseau, Diaz, and even Corot—but succeeded only in resembling questionable imitations.

"There's to be quite a week-end party?" inquired Querida.

"I don't know. My sister telephoned me to fill in. I fancy the party is for you."

"For *me!*" exclaimed Querida with delightful enthusiasm. "That is most charming of Mrs. Collis."

"They'll all think it charming of you. Lord, what a rage you've become and what a furor you've aroused! . . . And you deserve it," added Neville, coolly.

Querida looked at him, calm intelligence in his dark gaze; and understood the honesty of the comment.

"That," he said, "if you permit the vigour of expression, is damn nice of you, Neville. But you can afford to be generous to other painters."

"Can I?" Neville turned and gazed at Querida, gray eyes clear in their searching inquiry. Then he laughed a little and looked out over the sunny landscape.

Querida's olive cheeks had reddened a trifle.

Neville said: "What *is* the trouble with my work, anyway? Is it what some of you fellows say?"

Querida did not pretend to misunderstand:

"Isn't he a wonder," murmured Neville, venturing to release the thumb.

The young mother bent over, examining her off-spring in all the eloquent silence of pride unutterable. After a little while she said: "I've got to feed him. Go back to the others, Louis, and say I'll be down after a while."

He sauntered back through the comfortable but modest house, glancing absently about him on his way to the terrace, nodding to familiar faces among the servants, stopping to inspect a sketch of his own which he had done long ago and which his sister loved and he hated.

"Rotten," he murmured—"it has an innocence about it that is actually more offensive than stupidity."

On the terrace Stephanie Swift came over to him:

"Do you want a single at tennis, Louis? The others are hot for Bridge—except Gordon Collis—and he is going to dicker with a farmer over some land he wants to buy."

Neville looked at the others:

"Do you mean to say that you people are going to sit here all hunched up around a table on a glorious day like this?"

"We are," said Alexander Cameron, calmly break-ing the seal of two fresh packs. "You artists have nothing to do for a living except to paint pretty models, and when the week end comes you're in fine shape to caper and cut up didoes. But we business men are too tired to go galumphing over the greensward when Saturday arrives. It's a wicker chair and a 'high one,' and peaceful and improving cards for ours."

"Yes, that's the one—Valerie West, isn't it? *Is* it, Louis? You know her, of course."

Neville nodded coolly.

"Introduce me," murmured Cameron, spreading a ·pack for cutting. "Perhaps she'd like to see the Stock Exchange when I'm at my best."

"*Is* she such a beauty? Do you know her, too, Mr. Querida?" asked Rose Aulne.

Querida laughed: "I do. Miss West is a most engaging, most amiable and cultivated girl, and truly very beautiful."

"Oh! They *are* sometimes educated?" asked Stephanie, surprised.

"Sometimes they are even equipped to enter almost any drawing-room in New York. It doesn't always require the very highest equipment to do that," he added, laughing.

"That sounds like romantic fiction," observed Alice Annan. "You are a poet, Mr. Querida."

"Oh, it's not often a girl like Valerie West crosses our path. I admit that. Now and then such a comet passes across our sky—or is reported. I never before saw any except this one."

"If she's as much of a winner as all that," began Cameron with decision, "I want to meet her immediately——"

"Mere brokers are out of it," said Alice. . . . "Cut, please."

Rose Aulne said: "If you painters only knew it, your stupid studio teas would be far more interesting if you'd have a girl like this Valerie West to pour for you . . . and for us to see."

"Yes," added Alice; "but they're a vain lot. They

"'If she's as much of a winner as all that,' began Cameron with decision, 'I want to meet her immediately——'"

think we are unsophisticated enough to want to go to their old studios and be perfectly satisfied to look at their precious pictures, and listen to their art patter. I've told Harry that what we want is to see something of the real studio life; and he tries to convince me that it's about as exciting as a lawyer's life when he dictates to his stenographer."

"Is it?" asked Stephanie of Neville.

"Just about as exciting. Some few business men may smirk at their stenographers; some few painters may behave in the same way to their models. I fancy it's the exception to the rule in any kind of business— isn't it, Sandy?"

109

"Certainly," said Cameron, hastily. "I never winked at my stenographer—never! never! Will you deal, Mr. Querida?" he asked, courteously.

"I should think a girl like that would be interesting to know," said Lily Collis, who had come up behind her brother and Stephanie Swift and stood, a hand on each of their shoulders, listening and looking on at the card game.

"That is what I wanted to say, too," nodded Stephanie. "I'd like to meet a really nice girl who is courageous enough and romantic enough to pose for artists——"

"You mean poor enough, don't you?" said Neville. "They don't do it because it's romantic."

"It must be romantic work."

"It isn't, I assure you. It's drudgery—and sometimes torture."

Stephanie laughed: "I believe it's easy work and a gay existence full of romance. Don't undeceive me, Louis. And I think you're selfish not to let us meet your beautiful Valerie at tea."

"Why not?" added his sister. "I'd like to see her myself."

"Oh, Lily, you know perfectly well that oil and water don't mix," he said with a weary shrug.

"I suppose we're the oil," remarked Rose Aulne— "horrid, smooth, insinuating stuff. And his beautiful Valerie is the clear, crystalline, uncontaminated fountain of inspiration."

Lily Collis dropped her hands from Stephanie's and her brother's shoulders:

"Do ask us to tea to meet her, Louis," she coaxed. "We've never seen a model——"

plainly a few minutes ago I never clearly understood
that I couldn't marry Stephanie. When I thought of
it at all it seemed a vague and shadowy something, too

"'Come on, Alice, if you're going to scrub before luncheon.'"

far away to be really impending—threatening—like
death——"

"Oh!" cried his sister in revolt. "I shall make it
my business to see that Stephanie understands you thoroughly before this goes any farther——"

"I wish to heaven you would," he said, so heartily

" How do you keep up your game, Louis? Or do I never improve? It's curious, isn't it, that we are always deadlocked."

Bare-armed, bright hair in charming disorder, she swung along beside him with that quick, buoyant step so characteristic of a spirit ever undaunted, saluting the others on the terrace with high-lifted racquet.

" Nobody won," she said. " Come on, Alice, if you're going to scrub before luncheon. Thank you, Louis; I've had a splendid game—" She stretched out a frank hand to him, going, and the tips of her fingers just brushed his.

His sister gave him a tragic look, which he ignored, and a little later luncheon was on and Cameron garrulous, and Querida his own gentle, expressive, fascinating self, devotedly receptive to any woman who was inclined to talk to him or to listen.

That evening Neville said to his sister: " There's a train at midnight; I don't think I'll stay over——"

" Why? "

" I want to be in town early."

" Why? "

" The early light is the best."

" I thought you'd stopped painting for a while."

" I have, practically. There's one thing I keep on with, in a desultory sort of way——"

" What is it? "

" Oh, nothing of importance—" he hesitated—" that is, it may be important. I can't be sure, yet."

" Will you tell me what it is? "

" Why, yes. It's a portrait—a study——"

" Of whom, dear? "

" Oh, of nobody you know———"

" Is it a portrait of Valerie West? "

" Yes," he said, carelessly.

There was a silence; in the starlight his shadowy face was not clearly visible to his sister.

" Are you leaving just to continue that portrait? "

" Yes. I'm interested in it."

" Don't go," she said, in a low voice.

" Don't be silly," he returned shortly.

" Dear, I am not silly, but I suspect you are beginning to be. And over a model! "

" Lily, you little idiot," he laughed, exasperated; " what in the world is worrying you? "

" Your taking that girl to the St. Regis. It isn't like you."

" Good Lord! How many girls do you suppose I've taken to various places? "

" Not many," she said, smiling at him. " Your reputation for gallantries is not alarming."

He reddened. " You're perfectly right. That sort of thing never appealed to me."

" Then why does it appeal to you now? "

" It doesn't. Can't you understand that this girl is entirely different———"

" Yes, I understand. And that is what worries me."

" It needn't. It's precisely like taking any girl you know and like———"

" Then let me know her—if you mean to decorate public places with her."

They looked at one another steadily.

" Louis," she said, " this pretty Valerie is not your sister's sort, or you wouldn't hesitate."

" I—hesitate—yes, certainly I do. It's absurd on

the face of it. She's too fine a nature to be patronised
—too inexperienced in the things of your world—too
ignorant of petty conventions and formalities—too free
and fearless and confident and independent to appeal to
the world you live in."

" Isn't that a rather scornful indictment against my
world, dear? "

" No. Your world is all right in its way. You and
I were brought up in it. I got out of it. There are
other worlds. The one I now inhabit is more interesting
to me. It's purely a matter of personal taste, dear.
Valerie West inhabits a world that suits her."

" Has she had any choice in the matter? "

" I—yes. She's had the sense and the courage to
keep out of the various unsafe planets where electric
light furnishes the principal illumination."

" But has she had a chance for choosing a better
planet than the one you say she prefers? Your choice
was free. Was hers? "

" Look here, Lily! Why on earth are you so significant about a girl you never saw—scarcely ever
heard of——"

" Dear, I have not told you everything. I *have*
heard of her—of her charm, her beauty, her apparent
innocence—yes, her audacity, her popularity with men.
. . . Such things are not unobserved and unreported
between your new planet and mine. Harry Annan is
frankly crazy about her, and his sister Alice is scared
to death. Mr. Ogilvy, Mr. Burleson, Clive Gail, dozens
of men I know are quite mad about her. . . . If it was
she whom you used as model for the figures in the
Byzantine decorations, she *is* divine—the loveliest creature to look at! And I don't care, Louis; I don't care

120

drinker, no cruncher of macaroons, no gabbler at receptions, no top-hatted haunter of weddings, no social graduate of the Ecole Turvydrop. And these places — if I want to find companionship in any girl of your world — I must frequent. And I won't. And so there you are."

His sister came up to him and placed her arms around his neck.

"Such — a — wrong-headed — illogical — boy," she sighed, kissing him leisurely to punctuate her words. "If you marry a girl you love you can have all the roaming and unrestrained companionship you want. Did that ever occur to you?"

"At that price," he said, laughing, "I'll do without it."

"Wrong head, handsome head! I'm in despair about you. Why in the world cannot artists conform to the recognised customs of a perfectly pleasant and respectable world? Don't answer me! You'll make me very unhappy. . . . Now go and talk to Stephanie. The child won't understand your going to-night, but make the best of it to her."

"Good Lord, Lily! I haven't a string tied to me. It doesn't matter to Stephanie what I do — why I go or remain. You're all wrong. Stephanie and I understand each other."

"I'll see that she understands *you*," said his sister, sorrowfully.

He laughed and kissed her again, impatient. But why he was impatient he himself did not know. Certainly it was not to find Stephanie, for whom he started to look — and, on the way, glanced at his watch, determined not to miss the train that would bring him into town in time to talk to Valerie West over the telephone.

Passing the lighted and open windows, he saw Querida and Alice absorbed in a tête-à-tête, ensconced in a corner of the big living room; saw Gordon playing with Heinz, the dog—named Heinz because of the cele- brated "57 varieties" of dog in his pedigree — saw Miss Aulne at solitaire, exchanging lively civilities with Sandy Cameron at the piano between charming bits of a classic ballad which he was inclined to sing:

> "I'd share my pottage
> With you, dear, but
> True love in a cottage
> Is hell in a hut."

"Is that you, Stephanie?" he asked, as a dark fig- ure, seated on the veranda, turned a shadowy head toward him.

"Yes. Isn't this starlight magnificent? I've been up to the nursery looking at the infant wonder—just wild to hug him; but he's asleep, and his nurse glared at me. So I thought I'd come and look at something else as unattainable—the stars, Louis," she added, laughing—"not you."

"Sure," he said, smiling, "I'm always obtainable. Unlike the infant upon whom you had designs," he added, "I'm neither asleep nor will any nurse glare at you if you care to steal a kiss from me."

"I've no inclination to transfer my instinctively maternal transports to you," she said, serenely, "though maternal solicitude might not be amiss concerning you."

"Do you think I need moral supervision?"

"Not by me."

"By whom?"

123

"Well, then," he went on. "I take it for granted that our understanding is as delightfully thorough as it has always been—a warm, cordial intimacy which leaves us perfectly unembarrassed—perfectly free to express our affection for each other without fear of being misunderstood."

The girl lifted her blue eyes: "Of course."

"That's what I told Lily," he nodded, delighted. "I told her that you and I understood each other—that it was silly of her to suspect anything sentimental in our comradeship; that whenever the real thing put in an appearance and came tagging down the pike after you, you'd sink the gaff into him——"

"The—what?"

"Rope him and paste your monogram all over him."

"I certainly will," she said, laughing. Eyes and lips and voice were steady; but the tumult in her brain confused her.

"That is exactly what I told Lily," he said. "She seems to think that if two people frankly enjoy each other's society they want to marry each other. All married women are that way. Like clever decoys they take genuine pleasure in bringing the passing string under the guns."

He laughed and kissed her pretty fingers again:

"Don't you listen to my sister. Freedom's a good thing; and people are selfish when happy; they don't set up a racket to attract others into their private paradise."

"Oh, Louis, that is really horrid of you. Don't you think Lily is happy?"

"Sure—in a way. You can't have a perfectly

"I know."

Valerie plucked a grass blade and bit it in two reflectively.

"It's a funny sort of a world, isn't it, Rita?"

"Very humorous—if you look at it that way."

"Don't you?"

"Not entirely."

Valerie glanced up at the hammock.

"How did *you* happen to become a model, Rita?"

"I'm a clergyman's daughter; what do you expect?" she said, with smiling bitterness.

"*You!*" .

"From Massachusetts, dear. . . . The blue-light elders got on my nerves. I wanted to study music, too, with a view to opera." She laughed unpleasantly.

"Was your home life unhappy, dear?"

"Does a girl leave happiness?"

"You didn't run away, did you?" .

"I did—straight to the metropolis as a moth to its candle."

Valerie waited, then, timidly: "Did you care to tell me any more, dear? I thought perhaps you might like me to ask you. It isn't curiosity."

"I know it isn't—you blessed child! I'll tell you—some day—perhaps. . . . Pull the rope and set me swinging, please. . . . Isn't this sky delicious—glimpsed through the green leaves? Fancy you're not knowing the happiness of the country! I've always known it. Perhaps the trouble was I had too much of it. My town was an ancient, respectable, revolutionary relic set in a very beautiful rolling country near the sea; but I suppose I caught the infection—the country rolled, the breakers rolled, and finally I rolled out of

it all—over and over plump into Gotham! And I didn't
land on my feet, either. . . . You are correct, Valerie;
there is something humorous about this world. . . .
There's one of the jokes, now!" as a native passed,
hunched up on the dashboard, driving a horse and a
heifer in double harness.

"Shall we go to the post office with him?" cried
Valerie, jumping to her feet.

"Now, dear, what is the use of our going to the

"Valerie sat cross-legged on the grass . . . scribbling away."

145

post office when nobody knows our address and we
never could possibly expect a letter!"

"That is true," said Valerie, pensively. "Rita, I'm
beginning to think I'd like to have a letter. I believe—
I believe that I'll write to—to somebody."

"That is more than I'll do," yawned Rita, closing
her eyes. She opened them presently and said:

"I've a nice little writing case in my trunk. Sam
presented it. Bring it out here if you're going to
write."

The next time she unclosed her eyes Valerie sat
cross-legged on the grass by the hammock, the writing
case on her lap, scribbling away as though she really
enjoyed it.

The letter was to Neville. It ran on:

"Rita is asleep in a hammock; she's too pretty for
words. I love her. Why? Because she loves me, silly!

"I'm a very responsive individual, Kelly, and a pat
on the head elicits purrs.

"I want you to write to me. Also, pray be flattered;
you are the only person on earth who now has my address. I *may* send it to José Querida; but that is none
of your business. When I saw the new moon on the
stump-pond last night I certainly did wish for Querida
and a canoe. He can sing very charmingly.

"Now I suppose you want to know under what circumstances I have permitted myself to wish for you.
If you talk to a man about another man he always
attempts to divert the conversation to himself. Yes, he
does. And you are no better than other men, Louis—
not exempt from their vanities and cunning little weak-
nesses. Are you?

146

"How well you look!" he exclaimed, laughingly; "I never saw such a flawless specimen of healthy perfection!"

"'How well you look!' he exclaimed."

"Oh, I know I look like a milk-maid, Kelly; I've behaved like one, too. Did you ever see such a skin? Do you suppose this sun-burn will ever come off?"

"Instead of snow and roses you're strawberries and

cream," he said—" and it's just as fetching, Valerie.
How are you, anyway?"

" Barely able to sit up and take nourishment," she
admitted, demurely. ". . . I don't think you look particularly vigorous," she added, more seriously. " You
are brown but thin."

" Thin as a scorched pancake," he nodded. " The
ocean was like a vast plate of clam soup in which I
simmered several times a day until I've become as leath-
ery and attenuated as a punctured pod of kelp. . . .
Where's the rig we depart in, Valerie?" he concluded,
looking around the sun-scorched, wooden platform with
smiling interest.

" I drove down to meet you in a buck-board."

" Splendid! Is there room for my suit case?"

" Plenty. I brought yards of rope."

They walked to the rear of the station where buck-
board and horse stood tethered to a tree. He fastened
his suit case to the rear of the vehicle, swathing it se-
curely in fathoms of rope; she sprang in, he followed;
but she begged him to let her drive, and pulled on a
pair of weather-faded gloves with a business-like air
which was enchanting.

So he yielded seat and rusty reins to her; whip in
hand, she steered the fat horse through the wilderness of
arriving and departing carriages of every rural style
and description—stages, surreys, mountain-waggons,
buck-boards — drove across the railroad track, and
turned up a mountain road—a gradual ascent bordered
heavily by blackberry, raspberry, thimble berry and wild
grape, and flanked by young growths of beech and
maple set here and there with hemlock and white pine.
But the characteristic foliage was laurel and rhododen-

" How is the work going, Louis? " she asked, glancing at him askance.

" It's stopped."

" *À cause de——?* "

" *Je n'en sais rien, Valerie.*"

She flicked the harness with her whip, absently. He also leaned back, thoughtfully intent on the blue hills in the distance.

" Has not your desire to paint returned? "

" No."

" Do you know why? "

" Partly. I am up against a solid wall. There is no thoroughfare."

" Make one."

" Through the wall? "

" Straight through it."

" Ah, yes "—he murmured—" but what lies beyond? "

" It would spoil the pleasures of anticipation to know beforehand."

He turned to her: " You are good for me. Do you know it? "

" Querida said that, too. He said that I was an experience; and that all good work is made up of experiences that concern it only indirectly."

" Do you like Querida? " he asked, curiously.

" Sometimes."

" Not always? "

" Oh, yes, always more or less. But sometimes—" she was silent, her dark eyes dreaming, lips softly parted.

" What do you mean by that? " he inquired, carelessly.

the paper aside, and drew her pretty wrap around her shoulders.

"It's absurd," she said, plaintively, "but in this place I become horribly sleepy by nine o'clock. You won't mind if I go up, will you?"

"Not if you feel that way about it," he said, smiling.

"Oh, Rita!" said Valerie, reproachfully, "I thought we were going to row Louis about on the stump-pond!"

"I am too sleepy; I'd merely fall overboard," said Rita, simply, gathering up her bonbons. "Louis, you'll forgive me, won't you? I don't understand why, but that child never sleeps."

They rose to bid her good night. Valerie's finger tips rested a moment on Neville's sleeve in a light gesture of excuse for leaving him and of promise to return. Then she went away with Rita.

When she returned, the piazza was deserted except for Neville, who stood on the steps smoking and looking out across the misty waste.

"I usually go up with Rita," she said. "Rita is a dear. But do you know, I believe she is not a particularly happy girl."

"Why?"

"I don't know why. . . . After all, such a life—hers and mine—is only happy if you make it so. . . . And I don't believe she tries to make it so. Perhaps she doesn't care. She is very young—and very pretty—too young and pretty to be so indifferent—so tired."

She stood on the step behind and above him, looking down at his back and his well-set shoulders. They were inviting, those firm, broad, young shoulders of his; and she laid both hands on them.

Countess of Severn's new dressmaking drawing-rooms whither all snobdom crowded and shoved to get near the trade-marked coronet, and where bewildering young ladies strolled haughtily about all day long, displaying to agitated Gotham the most startling gowns in the extravagant metropolis.

She had other opportunities, too—such as meeting several varieties of fashionable men of various ages—gentlemen prominently identified with the arts and sciences—the art of killing time and the science of enjoying the assassination. And some of these assorted gentlemen maintained extensive stables and drove tandems, spikes, and fours; and some were celebrated for their yachts, or motors, or prima-donnas, or business acumen, or charitable extravagances. . . . Yes, truly, Valerie West was beginning to have many opportunities in this generously philanthropic world. And she was making a great deal of money—for her—but nothing like what she might very easily have made. And she knew it, young as she was. For it does not take very long to learn about such things when a girl is attempting to earn her living in this altruistic world.

" She'll spread her wings and go one of these days," observed Archie Allaire to Rita Tevis, who was posing as Psyche for one of his clever, thinly brushed, high-keyed studies very much after the manner and palette of Chaplin when they resembled neither Chartrain nor Zier, nor any other artist temporarily in vogue. For he was an adaptable man, facile, adroit, a master navigator in trimming sail to the fitful breeze of popular favour. And his work was in great demand.

" She'll be decorating the tonneau of some big touring car with crested panels—and there'll be a bunch

Among other minor incidents, almost local in character, the Academy and Society of American Artists opened its doors. And the exhibition averaged as well as it ever will, as badly as it ever had averaged. Allaire showed two portraits of fashionable women, done, this time, in the manner of Zorn, and quite as clever on the streaky surface. Sam Ogilvy proudly displayed another mermaid—Rita in the tub—and two babies from photographs and " chic "—very bad; but as usual it was very quickly marked sold.

Annan had a portrait of his sister Alice, poorly painted and even recognised by some of her more intimate friends. Clive Gail offered one of his marines— waves splashing and dashing all over the canvas so realistically that women instinctively stepped back and lifted their skirts, and men looked vaguely around for a waiter—at least Ogilvy said so. As for Neville, he had a single study to show—a full length—just the back and head and the soft contour of limbs melting into a luminously sombre background—a masterpiece in technical perfection, which was instantly purchased by a wise and Western millionaire, and which left the public staring but unmoved.

But it was José Querida who dominated the whole show, flooding everything with the splendour of his sunshine so that all else in the same room looked cold or tawdry or washed out. His canvas, with its superbly vigorous drawing, at once became the sensation of the exhibition. Sunday supplements reproduced it with a photograph of Querida looking amiably at a statuette of Venus which he held in his long, tapering fingers; magazines tried to print it in two colours, in three, in dozens, and made fireworks of it to Querida's inwardly

171

"Querida had laughed . . . and returned compliment for compliment."

—and he never found her at home; so he went South without hearing from her.

After he arrived, it is true, he received from her a cigarette case and a very gay and frank Christmas greeting—happy and untroubled apparently, brimming

175

with gossip, inconsequences, and nonsense. In it she thanked him for his letter and his gift, hoped he was happy with his parents, and expressed an almost conventional desire to see him on his return.

Then his parents came back to New York with him. Two days before New Year's Day they went to Spindrift House instead of sailing for Egypt, where for some years now they had been accustomed to spend the winters shivering at Shepherd's. And he and his sister and brother-in-law and Stephanie dined together that evening. But the plans they made to include him for a New Year's Eve home party remained uncertain as far as he was concerned. He was vague—could not promise —he himself knew not why. And they ceased to press him.

"You're growing thin and white," said Lily. "I believe you're getting painter's colic."

"House painters acquire that," he said, smiling. "I'm not a member of their union yet."

"Well, you must use as much white lead as they do on those enormous canvases of yours. Why don't you start on a trip around the world, Louis?"

He laughed.

Later, after he had taken his leave, the suggestion reoccurred to him. He took enough trouble to think about it the next morning; sent out his servant to amass a number of folders advertising world girdling tours of various attractions, read them while lunching, and sat and pondered. Why not? It might help. Because he certainly began to need help. He had gone quite stale. Querida was right; he ought to lie fallow. No ground could yield eternally without rest. Querida was clever enough to know that; and he had been stupid enough to

said, "I'm Mazie Gray. Nobody had the civility to tell you, did they?"

"They said something. . . . I'm Louis Neville," he replied, smiling.

"Are you?" she laughed. "Well, you may take it from mother that you're as cute as your name, Louis. Who was it they had all framed up to give me my cues? That big Burleson gentleman who'd starve if he had to laugh for a living, wasn't it? Can you laugh, child?"

"A few, Mazie. It is my only Sunday accomplishment."

"Dearie," she added, correcting him.

"It is my only accomplishment, dearie."

"That will be about all—for a beginning!" She laughed as the cab stopped at the red awning and Neville aided her to descend.

Steps, vestibules, stairs, cloak-rooms were crowded with jolly, clamouring throngs flourishing horns, canes, rattles, and dusters decked with brilliant ribbons. Already some bore marks of premature encounters with confetti and cocktails.

Waiters and head-waiters went gliding and scurrying about, assigning guests to tables reserved months in advance. Pages in flame-coloured and gold uniforms lifted the silken rope that stretched its barrier between the impatient crowd and the tables; managers verified offered credentials and escorted laughing parties to spaces bespoken.

Two orchestras, relieving each other, fiddled and tooted continuously; great mounds of flowers, smilax, ropes of evergreens, multi-tinted electroliers made the vast salon gay and filled it with perfume.

Even in the beginning it was lively enough though

not yet boisterous in the city where all New York was
dining and preparing for eventualities; the eventualities being that noisy mid-winter madness which seizes
the metropolis when the birth of the New Year is
imminent.

It is a strange evolution, a strange condition, a state
of mind not to be logically accounted for. It is not
accurate to say that the nicer people, the better sort,
hold aloof; because some of them do not. And in this
uproarious carnival the better sort are as likely to mis-
behave as are the worse; and they have done it, and
do it, and probably will continue to say and do and tolerate and permit inanities in themselves and in others
that, at other moments, they would regard as insanities
—and rightly.

Around every table, rosily illuminated, laughter
rang. White throats and shoulders glimmered, jewels
sparkled, the clear crystalline shock of glasses touching glasses rang continual accompaniment to the music
and the breezy confusion of voices.

Here and there, in premonition of the eventual, the
comet-like passage of streaming confetti was blocked
by bare arms upflung to shield laughing faces; arms
that flashed with splendid jewels on wrist and finger.

Neville, coolly surveying the room, recognised many,
responding to recognition with a laugh, a gesture, or
with glass uplifted.

"Stop making goo-goos," cried Mazie, dropping
her hand over his wrist. "Listen, and I'll be imprudent
enough to tell you the very latest toast—" She leaned
nearer, opening her fan with a daring laugh; but
Ogilvy wouldn't have it.

"This is no time for single sentiment!" he shouted. "Everybody should be perfectly plural to-night — everything should be plural, multiple, diffuse, all em-

Mazie Gray.

bracing, general, polydipsiatic, polygynyatic, polyandryatic!"

"What's polyandryatic?" demanded Mazie in astonishment.

"It means everybody is everybody else's! I'm yours and you're mine but everybody else owns us and we own everybody!"

"Hurrah!" shouted Annan. "Hear—hear! Where is the fair and total stranger who is going to steal the first kiss from me? Somebody count three before the rush begins——"

A ball of roses struck him squarely on the mouth; a furious shower of confetti followed. For a few moments the volleys became general, then the wild interchange of civilities subsided, and the cries of laughter died away and were lost in the loud animated hum which never ceased under the gay uproar of the music.

When they played the barcarole from Contes d'Hoffman everybody sang it and rose to their feet cheering the beautiful prima donna with whom the song was so closely identified, and who made one of a gay group at a flower-smothered table.

And she rose and laughingly acknowledged the plaudits; but they wouldn't let her alone until she mounted her chair and sang it in solo for them; and then the vast salon went wild.

Neville, surveying the vicinity, recognised people he never dreamed would have appeared in such a place —here a celebrated architect and his pretty wife entertaining a jolly party, there a well-known lawyer and somebody else's pretty wife; and there were men well known at fashionable clubs and women known in fashionable sets, and men and women characteristic of quieter sets, plainly a little uncertain and surprised to find themselves there. And he recognised assorted lights of the "profession," masculine and feminine; and one or two beautiful meteors that were falling athwart the underworld, leaving fading trails of incandescence in their jewelled wake.

The noise began to stun him; he laughed and talked

184

and sang with the others, distinguishing neither his own voice nor the replies. For the tumult grew as the hour advanced toward midnight, gathering steadily in strength, in license, in abandon.

And now, as the minute hands on the big gilded clock twitched nearer and nearer to midnight, the racket became terrific, swelling, roaring into an infernal din as the raucous blast of horns increased in the streets outside and the whistles began to sound over the city from Westchester to the Bay, from Long Island to the Palisades.

Sheer noise, stupefying, abominable, incredible, unending, greeted the birth of the New Year; they were dancing in circles, singing, cheering amid the crash of glasses. Table-cloths, silken gowns, flowers were crushed and trampled under foot; flushed faces looked into strange faces, laughing; eyes strange to other eyes smiled; strange hands exchanged clasps with hands unknown; the whirl had become a madness.

And, suddenly, in its vortex, Neville saw Valerie West. Somebody had set her on a table amid the silver and flowers and splintered crystal. Her face was flushed, eyes and mouth brilliant, her gown almost torn from her left shoulder and fluttering around the lovely arm in wisps and rags of silk and lace. Querida supported her there.

They pelted her with flowers and confetti, and she threw roses back at everybody, snatching her ammunition from a great basket which Querida held for her.

Ogilvy and Annan saw her and opened fire on her with a cheer, and she recognised them and replied with volleys of rosebuds—was in the act of hurling her last blossom—caught sight of Neville where he stood with

185

She looked at him in a confused, bewildered way—laid her hand on his sleeve with an impulse as though he had been about to strike her.

He no longer knew what he was doing in the sudden surge of unreasoning anger that possessed him; he shook her hand from his sleeve and turned.

And the next moment, on the stairs, she was beside him again, slender, pale, close to his shoulder, descending the great staircase beside him, one white-gloved hand resting lightly within his arm.

Neither spoke. At the cloak-room she turned and looked at him—stood a moment slowly tearing the orchids from her breast and dropping the crushed petals underfoot.

A maid brought her fur coat—his gift; a page brought his own coat and hat.

" Will you call a cab? "

He turned and spoke to the porter. Then they waited, side by side, in silence.

When the taxicab arrived he turned to give the porter her address, but she had forestalled him. And he entered the narrow vehicle; and they sat through the snowy journey in utter silence until the cab drew up at his door.

Then he said: " Are you not going home? "

" Not yet."

They descended, stood in the falling snow while he settled with the driver, then entered the great building, ascended in the elevator, and stepped out at his door.

He found his latch-key; the door swung slowly open on darkness.

CHAPTER VII

An electric lamp was burning in the hallway; he threw open the connecting doors of the studio where a light gleamed high on the ceiling, and stood aside for her to pass him.

She stepped across the threshold into the subdued radiance, stood for a moment undecided, then:

"Are you coming in?" she asked, cheerfully, quite aware of his ill-temper. "Because if you are, you may take off my coat for me."

He crossed the threshold in silence, and divested her of the fur garment which was all sparkling with melting snow.

"Do let's enjoy the firelight," she said, turning out the single ceiling lamp; "and please find some nice, big crackly logs for the fire, Kelly!—there's a treasure!"

His frowning visage said: "Don't pretend that it's all perfectly pleasant between us"; but he turned without speaking, cleared a big arm-chair of its pile of silks, velvets, and antique weapons, and pushed it to the edge of the hearth. Every movement he made, his every attitude was characterised by a sulky dignity which she found rather funny, now that the first inexplicable consternation of meeting him had subsided. And already she was wondering just what it was that had startled her; why she had left the café with him;

192

"I'd much prefer my own bed," she said, "if this is all you have to say to me."

"Had you anything to say to me?" he asked, unsmiling.

"About what, Kelly, dear?"

"God knows; I don't."

"Listen to this very cross and cranky young man!" she exclaimed, sitting up and winking her eyes in the rushing brilliancy of the blaze. "He is neither a very gracious host, nor a very reasonable one; nor yet particularly nice to a girl who left a perfectly good party for an hour with him."

She stole a glance at him, and her gaze softened:

"Perhaps," she said aloud to herself, "he is not really very cross; perhaps he is only tired—or in trouble. Otherwise his voice and manners are scarcely pardonable—even by me."

He stood regarding the flames with narrowing gaze for a few moments, then, hands in his pockets, walked over to his chair once more and dropped into it.

A slight flush stole into her cheeks; but it went as it came. She rose, crossed to where he sat and stood looking down at him.

"What *is* the matter?"

"With me?" in crude pretence of surprise.

"Of course. I am happy enough. What troubles *you?*"

"Absolutely nothing."

"Then—what troubles *us?*" she persisted. "What has gone wrong between us, Kelly, dear? Because we mustn't let it, you know," she added, slowly, shaking her head.

"Has anything gone wrong with us?" he asked, sullenly.

"Evidently. I don't know what it is. I'm keeping my composure and controlling my temper until I find out. You know what that dreadful temper of mine can be?" She added, smiling: "Well, then, please beware of it unless you are ready to talk sensibly. Are you?"

"What is it you wish me to say?"

"How perfectly horrid you can be!" she exclaimed. "I never knew you could be like this? Do you want a girl to go on her knees to you? I care enough for our friendship to do it—but I won't!"

Her mood was altering:

"You're a brute, Kelly, to make me miserable. I was having such a good time at the Gigolette when I suddenly saw you—your expression—and—I don't even yet know why, but every bit of joy went out of everything for me——"

"*I* was going out, too," he said, laughing. "Why didn't you remain? Your gay spirits would have returned untroubled after my departure."

There was an ugly sound to his laugh which checked her, left her silent for a moment. Then:

"Did you disapprove of me?" she asked, curiously. "Was that it?"

"No. You can take care of yourself, I fancy."

"I have had to," she said, gravely.

He was silent.

She added with a light laugh not perfectly genuine:

"I suppose I am experiencing with you what all mortals experience when they become entangled with the gods."

" That my friendship for you is as warm as the moment it began? "

He said, unsmiling: " People meet as we met, become friends—very good, very close friends—in that sort of friendship which is governed by chance and environment. The hazard that throws two people into each other's company is the same hazard that separates them. It is not significant either way. . . . I liked you—missed you. . . . Our companionship had been pleasant."

" Very," she said, quietly.

He nodded: " Then chance became busy; your duties led you elsewhere—mine set me adrift in channels once familiar——"

" Is that all you see in our estrangement? "

" What? " he asked, abruptly.

" Estrangement," she repeated, tranquilly. " That is the real word for it. Because the old intimacy is gone. And now we both admit it."

" We have had no opportunity to be together this——"

" We once *made* opportunities."

" We have had no time——"

" We halted time, hastened it, dictated to it, ruled it—once."

" Then explain it otherwise if you can."

" I am trying to—with God's help. Will you aid me, too? "

Her sudden seriousness and emotion startled him.

" Louis, if our estrangement is important enough for us to notice at all, it is important enough to analyse, isn't it? "

" I have analysed the reasons——"

I have loved you. And I do love you, dearly, honestly, cleanly, without other excuse than that, until to-night, you have been sweet to me and made me happier and better than I have ever been."

He sprang to his feet confused, deeply moved, suddenly ashamed of his own inexplicable attitude that seemed to be driving him into a bitterness that had no reason.

"Valerie," he began, but she interrupted him:

"I ask you, Kelly, to look back with me over our brief and happy companionship—over the hours together, over all you have done for me——"

"Have you done less for me?"

"I? What have I done?"

"You say you have given me—love."

"I have—with all my heart and soul. And, now that I think of it, I have given you more—I have given you all that goes with love—an unselfish admiration; a quick sympathy in your perplexities; quiet solicitude in your silences, in your aloof and troubled moments."
She leaned nearer,.a brighter flush on either cheek:

"Louis, I have given you more than that; I gave you my bodily self for your work—gave it to *you* first of all—came first of all to you—came as a novice, ignorant, frightened—and what you did for me then— what you were to me at that time—I can never, never forget. And that is why I overlook your injustice to me now!"

She sat up on the sofa's edge balanced forward between her arms, fingers nervously working at the silken edges of the upholstery.

"You ought never to have doubted my interest and affection," she said. "In my heart I have not

203

Her voice caught in her throat a moment; "I—such a matter has not occurred to me." She looked at him partly dismayed, partly confused, unable now to understand him—or even herself.

"You know—that kind of love—" she began—" *real* love, never has happened to me. You didn't think *that*, did you?—because—just because I did flirt a little with you? It didn't mean anything serious—anything of *that* kind. Kelly, dear, *have* you mistaken me? Is *that* what annoys you? Were you afraid I was silly enough, mad enough to—to really think of you—in that way?"

"No."

"Oh, I was sure you couldn't believe it of me. See how perfectly frank and honest I have been with you. Why, you never were sentimental—and a girl isn't unless a man begins it! You never kissed me—except last summer when you were going away—and both of our hearts were pretty full——"

"Wait," he said, suddenly exasperated, "are you trying to make me understand that you haven't the slightest real emotion concerning me—concerning me as a *man*—like other men?"

She looked at him, still confused and distressed, still determined he should not misunderstand her:

"I don't know what you mean; truly I don't. I'm only trying to make you believe that I am not guilty of thinking—wishing—of pretending that in our frank companionship there lay concealed anything of—of deeper significance——"

"Suppose—it were true?" he said.

"But it is *not* true!" she retorted angrily—and looked up, caught his gaze, and her breath failed her.

"Suppose it were true—for example," he repeated.
"Suppose you did find that you or I were capable of
—deeper——"

"Louis! Louis! Do you realise what you are saying to me? Do you understand what you are doing to
the old order of things between us—to the old confi-
dences, the old content, the happiness, the—the innocence of our life together? *Do* you? Do you even
care?"

"Care? Yes—I care."

"Because," she said, excitedly, "if it is to be—*that*
way with you—I—I can not help you—be of use to you
here in the studio as I have been. . . . *Am* I taking you
too seriously? You do not mean that you *really* could
ever love me, or I you, do you? You mean that
—that you just want me back again—as I was—as
we were—perfectly content to be together. That is
what you mean, isn't it, Kelly, dear?" she asked,
piteously.

He looked into her flushed and distressed face:

"Yes," he said, "that is exactly what I mean, Valerie—you dear, generous, clear-seeing girl! I just
wanted you back again; I miss you; I am perfectly
wretched without you, and that is all the trouble. Will
you come?"

"I—don't—know. Why did you say such a
thing?"

"Forgive me, dear!"

She slowly shook her head:

"You've made me think of—things," she said.
"You shouldn't ever have done it."

"Done what, Valerie?"

"What you did—what you said—which makes it

impossible for me to—to ever again be what I have been to you—even pose for you—as I did——"

"You mean that you won't pose for me any more?" he asked, aghast.

"Only—in costume." She sat on the edge of the sofa, head averted, looking steadily down at the hearth below. There was a pink spot on either cheek.

He thought a moment. "Valerie," he said, "I believe we had better finish what we have only begun to say."

"Is there—anything more?" she asked, unsmiling.

"Ask yourself. Do you suppose things can be left this way between us—all the happiness and the confidence—and the innocence, as you say, destroyed?"

"What more is there to say," she demanded, coldly.

"Shall—I—say it?" he stammered.

She looked up, startled, scarcely recognising the voice as his—scarcely now recognising his altered features.

"What *is* the matter with you!" she exclaimed nervously.

"Good God," he said, hoarsely, "can't you see I've gone quite mad about you!"

"About—*me!*" she repeated, blankly.

"About *you*—Valerie West. Can't you see it? Didn't you know it? Hasn't it been plain enough to you—even if it hasn't been to me?"

"Louis! Louis!" she cried in hurt astonishment, "what have you said to me?"

"That I'm mad about you, and I am. And it's been so—for months—always—ever since the very first! I must have been crazy not to realise it. I've been fool enough not to understand what has been the matter. Now you know the truth, Valerie!" He sprang to his feet, took a short turn or two before the hearth, then, catching sight of her face in its colourless dismay and consternation:

"I suppose you don't care a damn for me—that way!" he said, with a mirthless laugh.

"What!" she whispered, bewildered by his violence. Then: "Do you mean that you are in *love* with me!"

"Utterly, hopelessly—" his voice broke and he stood with hands clenched, unable to utter a word.

She sat up very straight and pale, the firelight gleaming on her neck and shoulders. After a moment his voice came back to his choked throat:

"I love you better than anything in the world," he said in unsteady tones. "And *that* is what has come between us. Do you think it is something we had better hunt down and destroy—this love that has come between us?"

"Is—is that *true?*" she asked in the awed voice of a child.

"It seems to be," he managed to say. She slid stiffly to the floor and stood leaning against the sofa's edge, looking at him wide-eyed as a schoolgirl.

"It never occurred to you what the real trouble might be," he asked, "did it?"

She shook her head mechanically.

"Well, we know now. Your court of inquiry has brought out the truth after all."

She only stared at him, fascinated. No colour had returned to her cheeks.

He began to pace the hearth again, lip caught savagely between his teeth.

"You are no more amazed than I am to learn the truth," he said. "I never supposed it was that. . . .

. . . Now that I look back and consider, I am sure of it."
She lifted her pretty head and gazed at him, then with
a gay little laugh of sheer happiness almost defiant:
"You see I am not afraid to love you," she said.

"Afraid? Why should you be?" he repeated,
watching her expression.

"Because—I am not going to marry you," she announced, gaily.

He stared at her, stunned.

"Listen, you funny boy," she added, framing his
face with her hands and smiling confidently into his
troubled eyes: "I am not afraid to love you because
I never was afraid to face the inevitable. And the inevitable confronts me now. And I know it. But I will
not marry you, Louis. It is good of you, dear of you
to ask it. But it is too utterly unwise. And I will not."

"Why?"

"Because," she said, frankly, "I love you better
than I do myself." She forced another laugh, adding:
"Unlike the gods, whom I love I do not destroy."

"That is a queer answer, dear——"

"Is it? Because I say I love you better than I do
myself? Why, Louis, all the history of my friendship
for you has been only that. Have you ever seen anything selfish in my affection for you?"

"Of course not, but——"

"Well, then! There isn't one atom of it in my love
for you, either. And I love you dearly—dearly! But
I'm not selfish enough to marry you. Don't scowl and
try to persuade me, Louis, I've a perfectly healthy mind
of my own, and you know it—and it's absolutely clear
on that subject. You must be satisfied with what I offer
—every bit of love that is in me—" She hesitated, level

"You say so many sweet, confusing, and foolish things to me, Louis, that while you are saying them I almost believe them. And then that clear, pitiless reasoning power of mine awakens me; and I turn my gaze inward and read written on my heart that irrevocable law of mine, that no unhappiness shall ever come to you through me."

Her face, sweetly serious, brightened slowly to a smile.

"Now I am going home, monsieur—home to think over my mad and incredible promise to you . . . and I'm wondering whether I'll wake up scared to death. . . . Daylight is a chilly shower-bath. No doubt at all that I'll be pretty well frightened over what I've said and done to-night. . . . Louis, dear, you simply *must* take me home this very minute!" She came up to him, placed both hands on his shoulders, kissed him lightly, looked at him for a moment, humorously grave:

"Some day," she said, "a big comet will hit this law-ridden, man-regulated earth—or the earth will slip a cog and go wabbling out of its orbit into interstellar space and side-wipe another planet—or it will ultimately freeze up like the moon. And who will care then *how* Valerie West loved Louis Neville?—or what letters in a forgotten language spelled 'wife' and what letters spelled 'mistress'? After all, I am not afraid of words. Nor do I fear what is in my heart. God reads it as I stand here; and he can see no selfishness in it. So if merely loving you all my life—and proving it—is an evil thing to do, I shall be punished; but I'm going to do it and find out what celestial justice really thinks about it."

221

petty disorder to your inspection than I would let you see me dress—even if we had been married for hundreds of years."

And still, on another occasion, when he had fought her for hours in an obstinate determination to make her say she would marry him—and when, beaten, chagrined, baffled, he had lost his temper, she won him back with her child-like candour and self-control.

"Your logic," he said, "is unbaked, unmature, unfledged. It's squab-logic, I tell you, Valerie; and it is not very easy for me to listen to it."

"I'm afraid that I am not destined to be entirely easy for you, dear, even with love as the only tie with which to bind you. The arbitrary laws of a false civilisation are going to impose on you what you think are duties and obligations to me and to yourself—until I explain them away. You must come to me in your perplexity, Louis, and give me a chance to remind you of the basic and proven proposition that a girl is born into this world as free as any man, and as responsible to herself and to others; and that her title to her own individuality and independence—her liberty of mind, her freedom to give and accept, her capability of taking care of herself, her divine right of considering, re-considering, of meeting the world unafraid—is what really ought to make her lovable."

He had answered: "What rotten books have you been reading?" And it annoyed her, particularly when he had asked her whether she expected to overturn, with the squab-logic of twenty years, the formalisms of a civilisation several thousand years old. He had added:

"The runways of wild animals became Indian paths;

position; never had his brushes swept with such sun-tipped fluency, never had the fresh splendour of his hues and tones approached so closely to convincing himself in the hours of fatigue and coldly sober reaction from the auto-intoxication of his own facility.

That auto-intoxication had always left his mind and his eye steady and watchful, although drugged—like the calm judgment of the intoxicated opportunist at the steering wheel of a racing motor. And a race once run and ended, a deliberate consideration of results usually justified the pleasure of the pace.

Yet that mysterious something which some said he lacked, had not yet appeared. That *something*, according to many, was an elusive quality born of a sympathy for human suffering—an indefinable and delicate bond between the artist and his world—between a master who has suffered, and all humanity who understands.

The world seemed to recognise this subtle bond between themselves and Querida's pictures. Yet in the pictures there was never any sadness. Had Querida ever suffered? Was it in that olive-skinned, soft-voiced young man to suffer?—a man apparently all grace and unruffled surface and gentle charm—a man whose placid brow remained smooth and untroubled by any line of perplexity or of sorrow.

And as Neville studied his own canvas coolly, logically, with an impersonal scrutiny that almost amounted to hostility, he wondered what it was in Querida's work that still remained absent in his. He felt its absence but he could not define what it was that was absent, could not discover the nature of it. He really began to feel the lack of it in his work, but he searched his canvas and his own heart in vain for any vacuum unfilled.

Then, too, had he himself not suffered? What had that restless, miserable winter meant, if it had not meant sorrow? He *had* suffered—blindly it is true until the

"He stood before it, searching in it for any hint of that elusive and mysterious *something*."

truth of his love for Valerie had suddenly confronted him. Yet that restless pain—and the intense emotion of their awakening—all the doubts, all the anxieties—the wonder and happiness and sadness in the imminence of that strange future impending for them both—had altered nothing in his work—brought into it no new quality—unless, as he thought, it had intensified to a dazzling brilliancy the same qualities which already had made his work famous.

" It's all talk," he said to himself—" it's sentimental jargon, precious twaddle—all this mysterious babble about occult quality and humanity and sympathy. If José Querida has the capacity of a chipmunk for mental agony, I've lost my bet that he hasn't."

And all the time he was conscious that there *was* something about Querida's work which made that work great; and that it was not in his own work, and that his own work was not great, and never had been great.

" But it will be," he said rather grimly to himself one day, turning with a shrug from his amazing canvas and pulling the unfinished portrait of Valerie into the cold north light.

For a long while he stood before it, searching in it for any hint of that elusive and mysterious *something*, and found none.

Moreover there was in the painting of this picture a certain candour amounting to stupidity—an uncertainty — a naïve, groping sort of brush work. It seemed to be technically, almost deliberately, muddled. There was a tentative timidity about it that surprised his own technical assurance—almost moved him to contempt.

What had he been trying to do? For what had he been searching in those slow, laborious, almost painful brush strokes—in that clumsy groping for values, in

Burleson said: " There's something honest and solid about it, anyway; hanged if there isn't."

" Like a hen," suggested Ogilvy, absently.

" Like a hen?" repeated Burleson. " What in hell has a hen got to do with the subject?"

" Like *you*, then, John," said Annan, " honest, solid, but totally unacquainted with the finer phases of contemporary humour——"

" I'm as humorous as anybody!" roared Burleson.

" Sure you are, John—just as humorously contemporaneous as anybody of our anachronistic era," said Ogilvy, soothingly. " You're right; there's nothing funny about a hen."

" And here's a highball for you, John," said Neville, concocting a huge one on the sideboard.

" And here are two charming ladies for you, John," added Sam, as Valerie and Rita Tevis entered the open door and mockingly curtsied to the company.

" We've dissected *your* character," observed Annan to Valerie, pointing to her portrait. "We know all about you now; Sam was the professor who lectured on you, but you can blame Kelly for turning on the searchlight."

" What search-light?" she asked, pivotting from Neville's greeting, letting her gloved hand linger in his for just a second longer than convention required.

" Harry means that portrait of you I started last year," said Neville, vexed. " He pretends to find it full of psychological subtleties."

" Do you?" inquired Valerie. " Have you discovered anything horrid in my character?"

" I haven't finished looking for the character yet," said Sam with an impudent grin. " When I find it I'll investigate it."

234

" Sam! Come here! "

He came carefully, wincing when she took him by the generous lobes of both ears.

" Now *what* did you say? "

" Help! " he murmured, contritely; " will no kind wayfarer aid me? "

" Answer me! "

" I only said you were beautifully decorative but intellectually impulsive—— "

" No, answer me, Sam! "

" Ouch! I said you had a pair of baby eyes and an obstinate mouth and an immature mind that came to conclusions before facts were properly assimilated. In other words I intimated that you were afflicted with incurable femininity and extreme youth," he added with satisfaction, " and if you tweak my ears again I'll kiss you! "

She let him go with a last disdainful tweak, gracefully escaping his charge and taking refuge behind Neville who was mixing another highball for Annan.

" This is a dignified episode," observed Neville, threatening Ogilvy with the siphon.

" Help me make tea, Sam," coaxed Valerie. " Bring out the table; that's an exceedingly nice boy. Rita, you'll have tea, too, won't you, dear? "

Unconsciously she had come to assume the role of hostess in Neville's studio, even among those who had been familiar there long before Neville ever heard of her.

Perfectly unaware herself of her instinctive attitude, other people noticed it. For the world is sharp-eyed, and its attitude is always alert, ears pricked forward even when its tail wags good-naturedly.

Ogilvy watched her curiously as she took her seat at the tea table. Then he glanced at Neville; but could not make up his mind.

It would be funny if there was anything between Valerie and Neville—anything more than there ever had been between the girl and dozens of her men friends. For Ogilvy never allowed himself to make any mistake concerning the informality and freedom of Valerie West in her intimacies with men of his kind. She was a born flirt, a coquette, daring, even indiscreet; but that ended it; and he knew it; and so did every man with whom she came in contact.

Yet—and he looked again at her and then at Neville —there seemed to him to be, lately, something a little different in the attitudes of these two toward each other —nothing that he could name—but it preoccupied him sometimes.

There was a little good-natured malice in Ogilvy; some masculine curiosity, too. Looking from Valerie to Neville, he said very innocently:

"Kelly, you know that peachy dream with whom you cut up so shamefully on New-year's night? Well, she asked me for your telephone number——"

"What are you talking about?" demanded Neville, annoyed.

"Why, I'm talking about Mazie," said Sam, pleasantly. "You remember Mazie Gray? And how crazy you and she became about each other?"

Valerie, who was pouring tea, remained amiably unconcerned; and Ogilvy obtained no satisfaction from her; but Neville's scowl was so hearty and unfeigned that a glimpse of his visage sent Annan into fits of laughter. To relieve which he ran across the floor, like

and most worthy, engaged Querida's attention for a while; but that intellectually lithe young man evaded the ponderously impending dispute with suave skill, and his gentle smile lingered longer on Valerie than on anybody else. Several times, with an adroit carelessness that seemed to be purposeless, he contrived to draw Valerie out of the general level of conversation by merely lowering his voice; but she seemed to understand the invitation; and, answering him as carelessly as he spoke, keyed her replies in harmony with the chatter going on around them.

He drank his tea smilingly; listened to the others; bore his part modestly; and at intervals his handsome eyes wandered about the studio, reverting frequently to the great canvas overhead.

"You know," he said to Neville, showing the eternal edge of teeth under his crisp black beard—"that composition of yours is simply superb. I am all for it, Neville."

"I'm glad you are," nodded Neville, pleasantly, "but it hasn't yet developed into what I hoped it might." His eyes swerved toward Valerie; their glances encountered casually and passed on. Only Rita saw the girl's breath quicken for an instant—saw the scarcely perceptible quiver of Neville's mouth where the smile twitched at his lip for its liberty to tell the whole world that he was in love. But their faces were placid, their expressions well schooled; Querida's half-veiled eyes appeared to notice nothing and for a while he remained smilingly silent.

Later, by accident, he caught sight of Valerie's portrait; he turned sharply in his chair and looked full at the canvas.

Nobody spoke for a moment; Neville, who was passing Valerie, felt the slightest contact as the velvet of her fingers brushed across his.

Then Querida rose and walked over to the portrait and stood before it in silence, biting at his vivid under lip and at the crisp hairs of his beard that framed it.

Without knowing why, Neville began to feel that Querida was finding in that half-finished work something that disturbed him; and that he was not going to acknowledge what it was that he saw there, whether of good or of the contrary.

Nobody spoke and Querida said nothing.

A mild hope entered Neville's mind that the *something*, which had never been in any work of his, might perhaps lie latent in that canvas—that Querida was discovering it—without a pleasure—but with a sensitive clairvoyance which was already warning him of a new banner in the distance, a new trumpet-call from the barriers, another lance in the lists where he, Querida, had ridden so long unchallenged and supreme.

Within him he felt a sudden and secret excitement that he never before had known—a conviction that the unexpressed hostility of Querida's silence was the truest tribute ever paid him—the tribute that at last was arousing hope from its apathy, and setting spurs to his courage.

Rita, watching Querida, yawned and concealed the indiscretion with her hand and a taunting word directed at Ogilvy, who retorted in kind. And general conversation began again.

Querida turned toward Neville, caught his eye, and shrugged:

"That portrait is scarcely in your happiest man-

same. But you misunderstood me. What was there in that silly conversation significant to you or to me other than an impersonal interest in hearing ideas expressed?"

"You knew I was in love with you."

"I did *not!*" she said, sharply.

"You let me touch your hands—kiss you, once——"

"And you behaved like a madman—and frightened me nearly to death! Had you better recall that night, José? I was generous about it; I was even a little sorry for you. And I forgave you."

"Forgave me my loving you?"

"You don't know what love is," she said, reddening.

"Do you, Valerie?"

She sat flushed and silent, looking fixedly at the cups and saucers before her.

"*Do* you?" he repeated in a curious voice. And there seemed to be something of terror in it, for she looked up, startled, to meet his long, handsome eyes looking at her out of a colourless visage.

"José," she said, "what in the world possesses you to speak to me this way? Have you any right to assume this attitude—merely because I flirted with you—as harmlessly—or meant it harmlessly——"

She glanced involuntarily across the studio where the others had gathered over the new collection of mezzotints, and at her glance Neville raised his head and smiled at her, and encountered Querida's expressionless gaze.

For a moment Querida turned his head away, and Valerie saw that his face was pale and sinister.

"José," she said, "are you insane to take our innocent affair so seriously? What in the world has

"'I shall have need of friends,' she said half to herself."

" Can you still like me? "

" Y-yes. Why, of course—if you'll let me."

" Shall we be the same excellent friends, Valerie?
And all this ill temper of mine will be forgotten? "

" I'll try. . . . Yes, why not? I *do* like you, and
I admire you tremendously."

His eyes rested on her a moment; he inhaled a deep
breath from his cigarette, expelled it, nodded.

They both were laughing now—he with apparent pleasure in her coquetry and animation, she still a little confused and instinctively on her guard.

Rita came strolling over, a tiny cigarette balanced between her slender fingers:

"Stop flirting, José," she said; "it's too near dinner time. Valerie, child, I'm dining with the unspeakable John again. It's a horrid habit. Can't you prescribe for me? José, what are you doing this evening?"

"Penance," he said; "I'm dining with my family."

"Penance," she repeated with a singular look—"well—that's one way of regarding the pleasure of having any family to dine with—isn't it, Valerie?"

"José didn't mean it that way."

Rita blew a ring from her cigarette's glimmering end.

"Will you be at home this evening, Valerie?"

"Y-yes . . . rather late."

"Too late to see me?"

"No, you dear girl. Come at eleven, anyway. And if I'm a little late you'll forgive me, won't you?"

"No, I won't," said Rita, crossly. "You and I are business women, anyway, and eleven is too late for week days. I'll wait until I can see you, sometime——"

"Was it anything important, dear?"

"Not to me."

Querida rose, took his leave of Valerie and Rita, went over and made his adieux to his host and the others. When he had gone Rita, standing alone with Valerie beside the tea table, said in a low voice:

"Don't do it, Valerie!"

"Do—what?" asked the girl in astonishment.

"Fall in love."

"Ogilvy stood looking sentimentally at the two young girls."

9

THE COMMON LAW

Valerie laughed.

"Do you mean with Querida?"

"No."

"Then—what *do* you mean?"

"You're on the edge of doing it, child. It isn't wise. It won't do for us. . . . I know—I *know*, Valerie, more than you know about—love. Listen to me. Don't! Go away—go somewhere; drop everything and go, if you've any sense left. I'll go with you if you will let me. . . . I'll do anything for you, dear. Only listen to me before it's too late; keep your self-control; keep your mind clear on this one thing, that love is of no use to us—no good to us. And if you think you suspect its presence in your neighbourhood, get away from it; pick up your skirts and run, Valerie. . . . You've plenty of time to come back and wonder what you ever could have seen in the man to make you believe you could fall in love with him."

Ogilvy, strolling up, stood looking sentimentally at the two young girls.

"A — perfect—pair — of precious — priceless — peaches," he said; "I'd love to be a Turk with an Oriental smirk and an ornamental dirk, and a tendency to shirk when the others go to work; for the workers I can't bear 'em and I'd rather run a harem——"

"No doubt," said Rita, coldly; "so you need not explain to me the rather lively young lady I met in the corridor looking for studio number ten——"

"Rita! Zuleika! Star of my soul! Jewel of my turban! Do you entertain suspicions——"

"Oh, *you* probably did the entertaining——"

"I? Heaven! How I am misunderstood! John Burleson! Come over here and tell this very charming

251

fered smilingly; the sordid struggle along the edges of starvation had hardened nothing of his heart.

Sensitive, sympathetic, ardent, proud, and ambitious with the quiet certainty of a man predestined, he had a woman's capacity for patience, for suffering, and for concealment, but not for mercy. And he cared passionately for love as he did for beauty—had succumbed to both in spirit oftener than in the caprice of some inconsequential amourette.

But never, until he came to know Valerie West, had a living woman meant anything vital to his happiness. Yet, what she aroused in him was that part of his nature to which he himself was a stranger—a restless, sensuous side which her very isolation and exposure to danger seemed to excite the more until desire to control her, to drive others away, to subdue, master, mould her, make her his own, obsessed him. And he had tried it and failed; and had drawn aside, fiercely, still watching and determined.

Some day he meant to marry properly. He had never doubted his ability to do so even in the sordid days. But there was no hurry, and life was young, and so was Valerie West—young enough, beautiful enough to bridge the years with him until his ultimate destiny awaited him.

And all was going well again with him until that New-year's night; and matters had gone ill with him since then—so ill that he could not put the thought of it from him, and her beauty haunted him—and the expression of Neville's eyes!——

But he remained silent, quiet, alert, watching and waiting with all his capacity for enduring. And he had now something else to watch—something that his sensitive intuition had divined in a single unfinished canvas of Neville's.

So far there had been but one man supreme in the new world as a great painter of sunlight and of women. There could not be two. And he already felt the approach of a shadow menacing the glory of his sunlight —already stood alert and fixedly observant of a young man who had painted something disquieting into an unfinished canvas.

That man and the young girl whom he had painted to the astonishment and inward disturbance of José Querida, were having no easy time in that new world which they had created for themselves.

Embarked upon an enterprise in the management of which they were neither in accord nor ever seemed likely to be, they had, so far, weathered the storms of misunderstandings and the stress of prejudice. Blindly confident in Love, they were certain, so far, that it was Love itself that they worshipped no matter what rites and ceremonies each one observed in its adoration. Yet each was always attempting to convert the other to the true faith; and there were days of trouble and of tears and of telephones.

Neville presented a frightfully complex problem to Valerie West.

His even-tempered indifference to others—an indifference which had always characterised him—had left only a wider and deeper void now filling with his passion for her.

They were passing through a maze of cross-purposes; his ardent and exacting intolerance of any creed and opinion save his own was ever forcing her toward a more formal and literal appreciation of what he was determined must become a genuine and formal engagement—which attitude on his part naturally produced clash after clash between them.

That he entertained so confidently the conviction of her ultimate surrender to convention, at moments vexed her to the verge of anger. At times, too, his disposition to interfere with her liberty tried her patience. Again and again she explained to him the unalterable fundamentals of their pact. These were, first of all, her refusal to alienate him from his family and his own world; second, her right to her own individuality and freedom to support herself without interference or unrequested assistance from him; third, absolute independence of him in material matters and the perfect liberty of managing her own little financial affairs without a hint of dependence on him either before or after the great change.

That she posed only in costume now did not satisfy him. He did not wish her to pose at all; and they discussed various other theatres for her business activity. But she very patiently explained to him that she found, in posing for interesting people, much of the intellectual pleasure that he and other men found in painting; that the life and the environment, and the people she met, made her happy; and that she could not expect to meet cultivated people in any other way.

" I *don't* want to learn stenography and take dictation in a stuffy office, dear," she pleaded. " I *don't* want to sit all day in a library where people whisper about books. I don't want to teach in a public school or read novels to invalids, or learn how to be a trained nurse and place thermometers in people's mouths. I like children pretty well but I don't want to be a governess and teach other people's children; I want to be taught myself; I want to learn—I'm a sort of a child, too, dear; and it's the familiarity with wiser people and brighter people and pleasant surroundings that has made me as happy as I am—given me what I never had as a child. You don't understand, but I'm having my childhood now—nursery, kindergarten, parties, boarding-school, finishing school, début—all concentrated into this happy year of being among gay, clever, animated people."

" Yet you will not let me take you into a world which is still pleasanter——"

And the eternal discussion immediately became inevitable, tiring both with its earnestness and its utter absence of a common ground. Because in him apparently remained every vital germ of convention and of generations of training in every precept of formality; and in her—for with Valerie West adolescence had arrived late—that mystery had been responsible for far-reaching disturbances consequent on the starved years of self-imprisonment, of exaltations suppressed, of fears and doubts and vague desires and dreams ineffable possessing the silence of a lonely soul.

And so, essentially solitary, inevitably lonely, out of her own young heart and an untrained mind she was evolving a code of responsibility to herself and to the world.

Her ethics and her morals were becoming what wide, desultory, and unrestrained reading was making them; her passion for happiness and for truth, her restless intelligence, were prematurely forming her character. There was no one in authority to tell her—check, guide,

261

"Understand what, dearest—dearest———"

"That I thought our love was its own protection—and mine."

He made no answer.

She knelt there silent for a little while, then put her hand up appealingly for his handkerchief.

"I have been very happy in loving you," she faltered; "I have promised you all there is of myself. And you have already had my best self. The rest—whatever it is—whatever happens to me—I have promised—so that there will be nothing of this girl called Valerie West which is not all yours—all, all—every thought, Louis, every pulse-beat—mind, soul, body. . . . But no future day had been set; I had thought of none as yet. Still—since I knew I was to be to you what I am to be, I have been very busy preparing for it—mind, soul, my little earthly possessions, my personal affairs in their small routine. . . . No bride in your world, busy with her trousseau, has been a happier dreamer than have I, Louis. You don't know how true I have tried to be to myself, and to the truth as I understand it—as true as I have been to you in thought and deed. . . . And, somehow, what threatened — a moment since — frightens me, humiliates me———"

She lifted her head and looked up at him with dimmed eyes:

"You were untrue to yourself, Louis—to your own idea of truth. And you were untrue to me. And for the first time I look at you, ashamed and shamed."

"Yes," he said, very white.

"Why did you offer our love such an insult?" she asked.

" My mercy, Louis? "

She rose to her knees and laid both hands on his shoulders.

" You *are* only a man, dear—with all the lovable faults and sins and contradictions of one. But there is no real depravity in you any more than there is in me. Only—I think you are a little more selfish than I am—you lose self-command—" she blushed—" but that is because you are only a man after all. . . . I think, perhaps, that a girl's love is different in many ways. Dear, my love for you is perfectly honest. You believe it, don't you? If for one moment I thought it was otherwise, I'd never let you see me again. If I thought for one moment that anything spiritual was to be gained for us by denying that love to you or to myself—or by living out life alone without you, I have the courage to do it. Do you doubt it? "

" No," he said.

She sighed, and her gaze passed from his and became remote for a moment, then:

" I want to live my life with you," she said, wistfully; " I want to be to you all that the woman you love could possibly be. But to me, the giving of myself to you is to be, in my heart, a ceremony more solemn than any in the world—and it is to be a rite at which my soul shall serve on its knees, Louis."

" Dearest—dearest," he breathed, " I know—I understand—I ask your pardon. And I worship you."

Then a swift, smiling change passed over her face; and, her hands still resting on his shoulders, kneeling there before him, she bent forward and kissed him on the forehead.

" Pax," she said. " You are forgiven. Love me

"But there's no use in *my* saying so if——"

"Oh, dear!" she exclaimed, "the great god totters on his pedestal and the oracle falters and I see·the mere man looking very humbly around the corner of the shrine at me, whispering, 'June, if you please, dear lady!'"

"Yes," he said, "that's what you see and hear. Now answer me, dear."

"And what am I to say?"

"June, please."

"June—please," she repeated, demurely.

"You darling! . . . What day?"

"Oh, that's too early to decide——"

"Please, dear!"

"No; I don't want to decide——"

"Dearest!"

"What?"

"Won't you answer me?"

"If you make me answer now, I'll be tempted to fix the first of April."

"All right, fix it."

"It's All Fool's·day, you know," she threatened. "Probably it is peculiarly suitable for us. . . . Very well, then, I'll say it."

She was laughing when he caught her hands and looked at her, grave, unsmiling. Suddenly her eyes filled with tears and her lip trembled.

"Forgive me, I meant no mockery," she whispered. "I had already fixed the first day of June for—for the great change in our lives. Are you content?"

"Yes." And before she knew what he was doing a brilliant flashed along her ring finger and clung sparkling to it; and she stared at the gold circlet and the gem flashing in the firelight.

There were tears in her eyes when she kissed it, looking at him while her soft lips rested on the jewel.

Neither spoke for a moment; then, still looking at him, she drew the ring from her finger, touched it again with her lips, and laid it gently in his hand.

"No, dear," she said.

He did not urge her; but she knew he still believed that she would come to think as he thought; and the knowledge edged her lips with tremulous humour. But her eyes were very sweet and tender as she watched him lay away the ring as though it and he were serenely biding their time.

"Such a funny boy," she said, "and such a dear one. He will never, never grow up, will he?"

"Such an idiot, you mean," he said, drawing her into the big chair beside him.

"Yes, I mean that, too," she said, impudently, nose in the air. "Because, if I were you, Louis, I wouldn't waste any more energy in worrying about a girl who is perfectly able to take care of herself, but transfer it to a boy who apparently is not."

"How do you mean?"

"I mean about your painting. Dear, you've got it into that obstinate head of yours that there's something lacking in your pictures, and there isn't."

"Oh, Valerie! You know there is!"

"No, no, no! There isn't anything lacking in them. They're all of you, Louis—every bit of you— as far as you have lived."

"What!"

"Certainly. As far as you have lived. Now live

272

a little more, and let more things come into your life. You can't paint what isn't in you; and there's nothing in you except what you get out of life."

She laid her soft cheek against his.

"Get a little real love out of life, Louis; a little *real* love. Then surely, surely your canvases can not disguise that you know what life means to us all. Love nobly; and the world will not doubt that love is noble; love mercifully; and the world will understand mercy. For I believe that what you are must show in your work, dear.

"Until now the world has seen in your work only the cold splendour, or dreamy glamour, or the untroubled sweetness and brilliancy of passionless romance. I love your work. It is happiness to look at it; it thrills, bewitches, enthralls! . . . Dear, forgive me if in it I have not yet found a deeper inspiration. . . . And that inspiration, to be there, must be first in you, my darling—born of a wider interest in your fellow men, a little tenderness for friends—a more generous experience and more real sympathy with humanity— and perhaps you may think it out of place for me to say it—but—a deeper, truer, spiritual conviction.

"Do you think it strange of me to have such convictions? I can't escape them. Those who are merciful, those who are kind, to me are Christ-like. Nothing else matters. But to be kind is to be first of all interested in the happiness of others. And you care nothing for people. You *must* care, Louis!

"And, somehow, you who are, at heart, good and kind and merciful, have not really awakened real love in many of those about you. For one thing your work has absorbed you. But if, at the same time, you could pay a little more attention to human beings——"

"Valerie!" he said in astonishment, "I have plenty of friends. Do you mean to say I care nothing for them?"

"How much *do* you care, Louis?"

"Why, I——" He fell silent, troubled gaze searching hers.

She smiled: "Take Sam, for example. The boy adores you. He's a rotten painter, I know—and you don't even pretend to an interest in what he does because you are too honest to praise it. But, Louis, he's a lovable fellow—and he does the best that's in him. You needn't pretend to care for what he does—but if you could show that you do care for and respect the effort——"

"I do, Valerie—when I think about it!"

"Then think about it; and let Sam know that you think about his efforts and himself. And do the same for Harry Annan. He's a worse painter than Sam—but do you think he doesn't know it? Don't you realise what a lot of heartache the monkey-shines of those two boys conceal?"

"I am fond of them," he said, slowly. "I like people, even if I don't show it——"

"Ah, Louis! Louis! That is the world's incurable hurt—the silence that replies to its perplexity—the wistful appeal that remains unanswered. . . . And many, many vex God with the desolation of their endless importunities and complaints when a look, a word, a touch from a human being would relieve them of the heaviest of all burdens—a sad heart's solitude."

He put his arm around her, impulsively:

" You little angel," he said, tenderly.

" No—only a human girl who has learned what solitude can mean."

" I shall make you forget the past," he said.

" No, dear—for that might make me less kind." She put her lips against his cheek, thoughtfully: " And —I think—that you are going to need all the tenderness in me—some day, Louis—as I need all of yours. . . . We shall have much to learn—after the great change. . . . And much to endure. And I think we will need all the kindness that we can give each other— and all that the world can spare us."

A painful colour flushed her face and neck; and at the same instant he realised what he had said.

Neither spoke for a while; he went on with his painting; she, standing once more for the full-length portrait, resumed her pose in silence.

After a while she heard his brushes clatter to the floor, saw him leave his easel, was aware that he was coming toward her. And the next moment he had dropped at her feet, kneeling there, one arm tightening around her knees, his head pressed close.

Listlessly she looked down at him, dropped one slim hand on his shoulder, considering him.

" The curious part of it is," she said, " that all the scorn in your voice was for Marianne Valdez and none for Penrhyn Cardemon."

He said nothing.

" Such a queer, topsy-turvy world," she sighed, letting her hand wander from his shoulder to his thick, short hair. She caressed his forehead thoughtfully.

" I suppose some man will say that of me some day. . . . But that is a little matter—compared to making life happy for you. . . . To be your mistress could never make me unhappy."

" To be your husband—and to put an end to all these damnable doubts and misgivings and cross-purposes would make me happy all my life!" he burst out with a violence that startled her.

" Hush, Louis. We must not begin that hopeless argument again."

" Valerie! Valerie! You are breaking my heart!"

" Hush, dear. You know I am not."

She looked down at him; her lip was trembling.

278

Suddenly she slid down to the floor and knelt there con-
fronting him, her arms around him.

"Dearer than all the world and heaven!—do you
think that I am breaking your heart? You *know* I am
not. You know what I am doing for your sake, for
your family's sake, for my own. I am only giving you
a love that can cause them no pain, bring no regret to
you. Take it, then, and kiss me."

But the days were full of little scenes like this—of
earnest, fiery discussions, of passionate arguments, of
flashes of temper ending in tears and heavenly recon-
ciliation.

He had gone for two weeks to visit his father and
mother at their summer home near Portsmouth, and
before he went he took her in his arms and told her how
ashamed he was of his bad temper at the idea of her
going on the *Mohave*, and said that she might go; that
he did trust her anywhere, and that he was trying to
learn to concede to her the same liberty of action and
of choice that any man enjoyed.

But she convinced him very sweetly that she really
had no desire to go, and sent him off to Spindrift House
happy, and madly in love; which resulted in two letters
a day from him, and in her passing long evenings in
confidential duets with Rita Tevis.

Rita had taken the bedroom next to Valerie's, and
together they had added the luxury of a tiny living
room to the suite.

It was the first time that either had ever had any
place in which to receive anybody; and now, delighted
to be able to ask people, they let it be known that their
friends could have tea with them.

279

Ogilvy and Annan had promptly availed themselves.

"This is exceedingly grand," said Ogilvy, examining everything in a tour around the pretty little sitting room. "We can have all kinds of a rough house now." And he got down on his hands and knees in the middle of the rug and very gravely turned a somersault.

"Sam! Behave! Or I'll set my parrot on you!" exclaimed Valerie.

Ogilvy sat up and inspected the parrot.

"You know," he said, "I believe I've seen that parrot somewhere."

"Impossible, my dear friend—unless you've been in my bedroom."

Ogilvy got up, dusted his trowsers, and walked over to the parrot.

"Well it looks like a bird I used to know—I—it certainly resembles—" He hesitated, then addressing the bird:

"Hello, Leparello—you old scoundrel!" he said, cautiously.

"Forget it!" muttered the bird, cocking his head and lifting first one slate-coloured claw from his perch, then the other;—"forget it! Help! Oh, very well. God bless the ladies!"

"*Where* on earth did you ever before see my parrot?" asked Valerie, astonished. Ogilvy appeared to be a little out of countenance, too.

"Oh, I really don't remember exactly where I did see him," he tried to explain; and nobody believed him.

"Sam! Answer me!"

"Well, where did *you* get him?"

"José Querida gave Leparello to me."

City. He was coming down, too, to stay a fortnight while I was there, and come back with me; and he said that he had intended to give the parrot to me after our return, but that he might as well give it to me before I went."

"I see," said Ogilvy, thoughtfully. A few moments later, as he and Annan were leaving the house, he said:

"It looks to me as though our friend, José, had taken too much for granted."

"It looks like it," nodded Annan, smiling unpleasantly.

"Too sure of conquest," added Ogilvy. "Got the frozen mitt, didn't he?"

"*And* the Grand Cordon of the double cross."

"*And* the hot end of the poker; yes?"

"Sure; and it's still sizzling." Ogilvy cast a gleeful glance back at the house:

"Fine little girl. All white. Yes? No?"

"All white," nodded Annan. . . . "And Neville isn't that kind of a man, anyway."

Ogilvy said: "So *you* think so, too?"

"Oh, yes. He's crazy about her, and she isn't taking Sundays out if it's his day in. . . . Only, what's the use?"

"No use. . . . I guess Kelly Neville has seen as many artists who've married their models as we have. Besides, his people are frightful snobs."

Annan, walking along briskly, swung his stick vigorously:

"She's a sweet little thing," he said.

"I know it. It's going to be hard for her. She can't stand for a mutt—and it's the only sort that will

282

counts and had now taken up her regular mending; and there she sat, sewing away, and singing in her clear, young voice, the old madrigal:

> *"Let us dry the starting tear*
> *For the hours are surely fleeting*
> *And the sad sundown is near.*
> *All must sip the cup of sorrow,*
> *I to-day, and thou to-morrow!*
> *This the end of every song,*
> *Ding-dong! Ding-dong!*
> *Yet until the shadows fall*
> *Over one and over all,*
> *Sing a merry madrigal!"*

Rita, nibbling a chocolate, glanced up:

"That's a gay little creed," she observed.

"Of course. It's the *only* creed."

Rita shrugged and Valerie went on blithely singing and sewing.

"How long has that young man of yours been away?" inquired Rita, looking up again.

"Thirteen days."

"Oh. Are you sure it isn't fourteen?"

"Perfectly." Then the sarcasm struck her, and she looked around at Rita and laughed:

"Of course I count the days," she said, conscious of the soft colour mounting to her cheeks.

Rita sat up and, tucking a pillow under her shoulders, leaned back against the foot-board of the bed, kicking the newspaper to the floor. "Do you know," she said, "that you have come pretty close to falling in love with Kelly Neville?"

"She and Rita dined with him once or twice."

father before him had left the grandfathers of these friends as legacies to his son.

It was a pallid and limited society that Henry Neville and his wife frequented—a coterie of elderly, intellectual people, and their prematurely dried-out offspring. And intellectual in-breeding was thinning it to attenuation—to a bloodless meagreness in which they, who composed it, conceived a mournful pride.

Old New Yorkers all, knowing no other city, no other bourne north of Tenth Street or west of Chelsea—silent, serene, drab-toned people, whose drawing-rooms were musty with what had been fragrance once, whose science, religion, interests, desires were the beliefs, interests and emotions of a century ago, their colourless existence and passive snobbishness affronted nobody who did not come seeking affront.

To them Theodore Thomas had been the last conductor; his orchestra the last musical expression fit for a cultivated society; the Academy of Music remained their last symphonic temple, Wallack's the last refuge of a drama now dead for ever.

Delmonico's had been their northern limit, Stuyvesant Square their eastern, old Trinity their southern, and their western, Chelsea. Outside there was nothing. The blatancy and gilt of the million-voiced metropolis fell on closed eyes, and on ears attuned only to the murmurs of the past. They lived in their ancient houses and went abroad and summered in some simple old-time hamlet hallowed by the headstones of their grandsires, and existed as meaninglessly and blamelessly as the old catalpa trees spreading above their dooryards.

And into this narrow circle Louis Neville and his sister Lily had been born.

It had been a shock to her parents when Lily married Gordon Collis, a mining engineer from Denver. She came to see them with her husband every year; Collis loved her enough to endure it.

As for Louis' career, his achievements, his work, they regarded it without approval. Their last great painters had been Bierstadt and Hart, their last great sculptor, Powers. Blankly they gazed upon the splendours of the mural symphonies achieved by the son and heir of all the Nevilles; they could not comprehend the art of the Uitlanders; their comment was silence and dignity.

To them all had become only shadowy tradition; even affection and human emotion, and the relationship of kin to kin, of friend to friend, had become only part of a negative existence which conformed to precedent, temporal and spiritual, as written in the archives of a worn-out civilisation.

So, under the circumstances, it was scarcely to be wondered that Neville hesitated to introduce the subject of Valerie West as he sat in the parlour at Spindrift House with his father and mother, reading the *Tribune* or the *Evening Post* or poring over some ancient tome of travels, or looking out across the cliffs at an icy sea splintering and glittering against a coast of frozen adamant.

At length he could remain no longer; commissions awaited him in town; hunger for Valerie gnawed ceaselessly, unsubdued by his letters or by hers to him.

" Mother," he said, the evening before his departure, "would it surprise you very much if I told you that I wished to marry?"

"No," she said, tranquilly; "you mean Stephanie Swift, I suppose."

"Tall, transparently pale, negative in character."

His father glanced up over his spectacles, and he hesitated; then, as his father resumed his reading:

"I don't mean Stephanie, mother."

His father laid aside his book and removed the thin gold-rimmed spectacles.

" I understand from Lily that we are to be prepared to receive Stephanie Swift as your affianced wife," he said. " I shall be gratified. Stephen Swift was my oldest friend."

" Lily was mistaken, father. Stephanie and I are merely very good friends. I have no idea of asking her to marry me."

" I had been given to understand otherwise, Louis. I am disappointed."

Louis Neville looked out of the window, considering, yet conscious of the hopelessness of it all.

" Who is this girl, Louis? " asked his mother, pulling the white-and-lilac wool shawl closer around her thin shoulders.

" Her name is Valerie West."

" One of the Wests of West Eighth Street? " demanded his father.

The humour of it all twitched for a moment at his son's grimly set jaws, then a slight flush mantled his face:

" No, father."

" Do you mean the Chelsea Wests, Louis? "

" No."

" Then we—don't know them," concluded his father with a shrug of his shoulders, which dismissed many, many things from any possibility of further discussion. But his mother's face grew troubled.

" Who is this Miss West? " she asked in a colourless voice.

" She is a very good, very noble, very cultivated, very beautiful young girl—an orphan—who is supporting herself by her own endeavours."

" What! " said his father, astonished.

And so he went away from Spindrift House
through a snow-storm, and arrived in New York late
that evening; but not too late to call Valerie on the
telephone and hear again the dear voice with its happy
little cry of greeting—and the promise of to-morrow's
meeting before the day of duty should begin.

Love grew as the winter sped glittering toward the
far primrose dawn of spring; work filled their days;
evening brought the happiness of a reunion eternally
charming in its surprises, its endless novelty. New,
forever new, love seemed; and youth, too, seemed immortal.

On various occasions when Valerie chanced to be at
his studio, pouring tea for him, friends of his sister
came unannounced—agreeable women more or less
fashionable, who pleaded his sister's sanction of an unceremonious call to see the great painted frieze before
it was sent to the Court House.

He was perfectly nice to them; and Valerie was
perfectly at ease; and it was very plain that these people were interested and charmed with this lovely Miss
West, whom they found pouring tea in the studio of an
artist already celebrated; and every one of them expressed themselves and their curiosity to his sister,
Mrs. Collis, who, never having heard of Valerie West,
prudently conveyed the contrary in smiling but silent
acquiescence, and finally wrote to her brother and told
him what was being said.

Before he determined to reply, another friend—or
rather acquaintance of the Collis family—came in to see
the picture—the slim and pretty Countess d'Enver.
And went quite mad over Valerie—so much so that she

301

—not originality. Its devotees were the devotees of Richard Strauss, of Huysmans, of Manet, of Degas, Rops, Louis Le Grand, Forain, Monticelli; its painters painted nakedness in footlight effects with blobs for faces and blue shadows where they were needed to conceal the defects of impudent drawing; its composers maundered with both ears spread wide for stray echoes of Salome; its sculptors, stupefied by Rodin, achieved sections of human anatomy protruding from lumps of clay and marble; its dramatists, drugged by Mallarmé and Maeterlinck, dabbled in dullness, platitude and mediocre psychology; its writers wrote as bloodily, as squalidly, and as immodestly as they dared; its poets blubbered with Verlaine, spat with Aristide Bruant, or leered with the alcoholic muses of the Dead Rat.

They were all young, all in deadly earnest, all imperfectly educated, all hard workers, brave workers, blind, incapable workers sweating and twisting and hammering in their impotence against the changeless laws of truth and beauty. With them it was not a case of a loose screw; all screws had been tightened so brutally that the machinery became deadlocked. They were neither lazy, languid, nor precious; they only thought they knew how and they didn't. All their vigour was sterile; all their courage vain.

Several attractive women exquisitely gowned were receiving; there was just a little something unusual in their prettiness, in their toilets; and also a little something lacking; and its absence was as noticeable in them as it was in the majority of arriving or departing guests.

It could not have been self-possession and breeding which an outsider missed. For the slim Countess d'En-

"Her poise, her unconsciousness, the winning simplicity of her manner were noticed

understand how intelligent people can even think about such things."

"Modernity," repeated Neville. "Hello; there's Carrillo, the young apostle of Bruant, who makes such a hit with the elect."

"How, Kelly?"

"Realism, New York, and the spade business. He saw a sign on a Bowery clothing store,—'Gents Pants Half Off Today,' and he wrote a poem on it and all Manhattan sat up and welcomed him as a peerless realist; and dear old Dean Williams compared him to Tolstoy and Ed. Harrigan, and there was the deuce to pay artistically and generally. Listen to the Yankee Steinlen in five-minute verse, dear."

Carrillo rose, glanced carelessly at his type-written manuscript and announced its title unconcernedly:

"Mutts In Madison Square.

"A sodden tramp sits scratching on a bench,
The S. C. D. cart trails a lengthening stench
Where White Wings scrape the asphalt; and a
    breeze
Ripples the fountain and the budding trees.
Now fat old women, waddling like hogs,
Arrive to exercise their various dogs;
And 'round and 'round the little mutts all run,
Grass-maddened, frantic, circling in the sun,
Wagging and nosing—see! beneath yon tree
One little mutt meets his affinity!
And, near, another madly wags his tail
Inquiringly; but his advances fail,
And, 'yap-yap-yap!' replies the shrewish tyke,
So off the other starts upon a hike,

310

Rushing at random, crazed with sun and air,
Circling and barking out his canine prayer:

"'Oh, Lord of dogs who made the Out-of-doors
And fashioned mutts to gambol on all fours,
Grant us a respite from the city's stones!
Grant us a grassy place to bury bones!—
A grassy spot to roll on now and then,
Oh, Lord of dogs who also fashioned men,
Accept our thanks for this brief breath of air,
And grant, Oh, Lord, a humble mongrel's prayer!'

. . . .

The hoboe, sprawling, scratches in the sun;
While 'round and 'round the happy mongrels run."

"Good Heavens," breathed Neville, "that sort of thing may be modern and strong, but it's too rank for me, Valerie. Shall we bolt?"

"I—I think we'd better," she said miserably. "I don't think I care for—for these interesting people very much."

They rose and passed slowly along the walls of the room, which were hung with "five-minute sketches," which probably took five seconds to conceive and five hours to execute—here an unclothed woman, chiefly remarkable for an extraordinary development of adipose tissue and house-maid's knee; here a pathological gem that might have aptly illustrated a work on malformations; yonder a dashing dab of balderdash, and next it one of Rackin's masterpieces, flanked by a gem of Stanley Pooks.

In the centre of the room, emerging from a chunk of marble, the back and neck and one ear of an un-

and of divinity was in that face; in the exquisitely sensitive wisdom of the woman's eyes, in the full sweet innocence of the childish mouth—in the smooth little

"'Where do you keep those pretty models, Louis?' he demanded."

hands so unsoiled, so pure—in the nun-like pallor and slender beauty of the throat.

Whatever had been his inspiration—whether spiritual conviction, or the physical beauty of Valerie, neither he nor she considered very deeply. But that he was embodying and creating something of the existence of which neither he nor she had been aware a

month ago, was awaking something within them that
had never before stirred or given sign of life.

Since the last section of the mural decoration for
the new court house had been shipped to its destination,
he had busied himself on two canvases, a portrait of his
sister in furs, and the portrait of Valerie.

Lily Collis came in the mornings twice a week to sit
for him; and once or twice Stephanie Swift came with
her; also Sandy Cameron, ruddy, bald, jovial, scoffing,
and insatiably curious.

"Where do you keep all those pretty models,
Louis?" he demanded, prying aside the tapestry with
the crook of his walking stick, and peeping behind furniture and hangings and big piles of canvases. "Be
a sport and introduce us; Stephanie wants to see a few
as well as I do."

Neville shrugged and went on painting, which exasperated Cameron.

"It's a fraud," he observed, in a loud, confidential
aside to Stephanie; "this studio ought to be full of
young men in velvet coats and bunchy ties, singing,
'Oh la—la!' and dextrously balancing on their baggy
knees a series of assorted soubrettes. It's a bluff, a
hoax, a con game! Are you going to stand for it?
I don't see any absinthe either—or even any Vin ordi-
naire! Only a tea-pot—a *tea-pot!*" he repeated in unutterable scorn. "Why, there's more of Bohemia in a
Broad Street Trust Company than there is in this Pull-
man car studio!"

Mrs. Collis was laughing so that her brother had
difficulty in going on with her portrait.

"Get out of here, Sandy," he said—"or take

Stephanie into the rest of the apartment, somewhere, and tell her your woes."

Stephanie, who had been exploring, turning over piles of chassis and investigating canvases and charcoal studies stacked up here and there against the wainscot, pulled aside an easel which impeded her progress, and in so doing accidentally turned the canvas affixed to it toward the light.

"Hello!" exclaimed Cameron briskly, "who is this?"

Lily turned her small, aristocratic head, and Stephanie looked around.

"What a perfectly beautiful girl!" she exclaimed impulsively; "who is she, Louis?"

"A model," he said calmly; but the careless and casual exposure of the canvas had angered him so suddenly that his own swift emotion astonished him.

Lily had risen from her seat, and now stood looking fixedly at the portrait of Valerie West, her furs trailing from one shoulder to the chair.

"My eye and Betty Martin!" cried Cameron, "I'll take it all back, girls! It's a real studio after all— and this is the real thing! Louis, do you think she's seen the Aquarium? I'm disengaged after three o'clock——"

He began to kiss his hand rapidly in the direction of the portrait, and then, fondly embracing his own walking stick, he took a few jaunty steps in circles, singing "Waltz me around again, Willy."

Lily Collis said: "If your model is as lovely as her portrait, Louis, she is a real beauty. "Who is she?"

"A professional model." He could scarcely contain his impatience with his sister, with Cameron's fat

317

" I don't think I know exactly why—unless the portrait was a personal and private affair concerning only
myself——"

" Louis! Has it gone as far as that? "

" As far as what? What on earth are you trying
to say, Lily? "

" I'm trying to say—as nicely and as gently as I
can—that your behaviour—in regard to this girl is
making us all perfectly wretched."

" Who do you mean by ' us all '? " he demanded
sullenly.

" Father and mother and myself. You must have
known perfectly well that father would write to me
about what you told him at Spindrift House a month
ago."

" Did he? "

" Of course he did, Louis! Mother is simply
worrying herself ill over you; father is incredulous—
at least he pretends to be; but he has written me twice
on the subject—and I think you might just as well
be told what anxiety and unhappiness your fascination
for this girl is causing us all."

Mrs. Collis was leaning far forward in her chair,
forgetful of her pose; Neville stood silent, head lowered,
absently mixing tints upon his palette without regard
to the work under way.

When he had almost covered his palette with useless
squares of colour he picked up a palette-knife, scraped
it clean, smeared the residue on a handful of rags, laid
aside brushes and palette, and walked slowly to the
window.

It was snowing again. He could hear the feathery
whisper of the flakes falling on the glass roof above;

fashion. But, dear, is that all that you, a Neville, require of the woman who is to bear your name—bear your children?"

"She *is* all I require—and far more."

"Dear, you are utterly blinded by your infatuation!"

"You do not know her."

"Then let me!" exclaimed Mrs. Collis desperately. "Let me meet her, Louis—let me talk with her——"

"No. . . . And I'll tell you why, Lily; it's because she does not care to meet you."

"What!"

"I have told you the plain truth. She sees no reason for knowing you, or for knowing my parents, or any woman in a world that would never tolerate her, never submit to her entrance, never receive her as one of them! — a world that might shrug and smile and endure her as my wife—and embitter my life forever."

As he spoke he was not aware that he merely repeated Valerie's own words; he remained still unconscious that his decision was in fact merely her decision; that his entire attitude had become hers because her nature and her character were as yet the stronger.

But in his words his sister's quick intelligence perceived a logic and a conclusion entirely feminine and utterly foreign to her brother's habit of mind. And she realised with a thrill of fear that she had to do, not with her brother, but with a woman who was to be reckoned with.

"Do you—or does Miss West think it likely that I am a woman to wound, to affront another—no matter who she may be? Surely, Louis, you could have told her very little about me——" ·

" I never mention you to her."

Lily caught her breath.

" Why? "

" Why should I? "

" That is unfair, Louis! She has the right to know about your own family—otherwise how can she understand the situation? "

" It's like all situations, isn't it? You and father and mother have your own arbitrary customs and traditions and standards of respectability. You rule out whom you choose. Valerie West knows perfectly well that you would rule her out. Why should she give you the opportunity? "

" Is she afraid of me? "

He smiled: " I don't think so. " And his smile angered his sister.

" Very well," she said, biting her lip.

For a few moments she sat there deliberating, her pointed patent-leather toe tapping the polished floor. Then she stood up, with decision:

" There is no use in our quarrelling, Louis—until the time comes when some outsider forces us into an unhappy misunderstanding. Kiss me good-bye, dear."

She lifted her face; he kissed her; and her hand closed impulsively on his arm:

" Louis! Louis! I love you. I am so proud of you—I—you know I love you, don't you? "

" Yes—I think so."

" You *know* I am devoted to your happiness! — your *real* happiness—which those blinded eyes in that obstinate head of yours refuse to see. Believe me—believe me, dear, that your *real* happiness is not in this pretty, strange girl's keeping. No, no, no! You

wardly Lily was pleasantly reserved, perfectly at ease with this young girl; inwardly all was commotion approaching actual consternation.

She had been prepared for youth, for a certain kind of charm and beauty—but not for this kind—not for the loveliness, the grace, the composure, the exquisite simplicity of this young girl who sat sewing there before her.

She was obliged to force herself to recollect that this girl was a model hired to pose for men—paid to expose her young, unclothed limbs and body! Yet— could it be possible! Was this the girl hailed as a comrade by the irrepressible Ogilvy and Annan—the heroine of a score of unconventional and careless gaieties recounted by them? Was this the coquette who, it was rumoured, had flung over Querida, snapped her white fingers at Penrhyn Cardemon, and laughed disrespectfully at a dozen respected pillars of society, who appeared to be willing to support her in addition to the entire social structure?

Very quietly the girl raised her head. Her sensitive lips were edged with a smile, but there was no mirth in her clear eyes:

"Mrs. Collis, perhaps you are waiting for me to say something about your letter and my answer to it. I did not mean to embarrass you by not speaking of it, but I was not certain that the initiative lay with me."

Lily reddened: "It lies with *me*, Miss West—the initiative. I mean—" She hesitated, suddenly realising how difficult it had become to go on,—how utterly unprepared she was to encounter passive resistance from such composure as this young girl already displayed.

"You wrote to me about your anxiety concerning Mr. Neville," said Valerie, gently.

"Yes—I did, Miss West. You will surely understand—and forgive me—if I say to you that I am still a prey to deepest anxiety."

"Why?"

The question was so candid, so direct that for a moment Lily remained silent. But the dark, clear, friendly eyes were asking for an answer, and the woman of the world who knew how to meet most situations and how to dominate them, searched her experience in vain for the proper words to use in this one.

After a moment Valerie's eyes dropped, and she resumed her sewing; and Lily bit her lip and composed her mind to its delicate task:

"Miss West," she said, "what I have to say is not going to be very agreeable to either of us. It is going to be painful perhaps—and it is going to take a long while to explain——"

"It need not take long," said Valerie, without raising her eyes from her stitches; "it requires only a word to tell me that you and your father and mother do not wish your brother to marry me."

She looked up quietly, and her eyes met Lily's:

"I promise not to marry him," she said. "You are perfectly right. He belongs to his own family; he belongs in his own world."

She looked down again at her sewing with a faint smile:

"I shall not attempt to enter that world as his wife, Mrs. Collis, or to draw him out of it. . . . And I hope that you will not be anxious any more."

She laid aside her work and rose to her slender

came in breezily to join her at luncheon she was ready, her costume mended and folded in her hand-satchel, and there remained scarcely even a redness of the lids to betray her.

That evening she did not stop for tea at Neville's studio; and, later, when he telephoned, asking her to dine with him, she pleaded the feminine prerogative of tea in her room and going to bed early for a change. But she lay awake until midnight trying to think out a *modus vivendi* for Neville and herself which would involve no sacrifice on his part and no unhappiness for anybody except, perhaps, for herself.

The morning was dull and threatened rain, and she awoke with a slight headache, remembering that she had dreamed all night of weeping.

In her mail there was a note from Querida asking her to stop for a few moments at his studio that afternoon, several business communications, and a long letter from Mrs. Collis which she read lying in bed, one hand resting on her aching temples:

"MY DEAR MISS WEST: Our interview this morning has left me with a somewhat confused sense of indebtedness to you and an admiration and respect for your character which I wished very much to convey to you this morning, but which I was at a loss to express.

"You are not only kind and reasonable, but so entirely unselfish that my own attitude in this unhappy matter has seemed to me harsh and ungracious.

"I went to you entertaining a very different idea of you, and very different sentiments from the opinion which I took away with me. I admit that my call on you was not made with any agreeable anticipations;

old, and they will never change in their beliefs and prejudices inherited from their parents, who, in turn, inherited their beliefs.

"It was for them more than for myself—more even than for my brother—that I appealed to you. The latter end of their lives should not be made unhappy. And your generous decision assures me that it will not be made so.

"As for myself, my marriage permitted me an early enfranchisement from the obsolete conventional limits within which my brother and I were brought up.

"I understand enough of the modern world not to clash with it unnecessarily, enough of ultra-modernity not to be too much afraid of it.

"But even I, while I might theoretically admit and even admire that cheerful and fearless courage which makes it possible for such a self-respecting woman as yourself to face the world and force it to recognise her right to earn her own living as she chooses—I could not bring myself to contemplate with equanimity my brother's marrying you. And I do not believe my father would survive such an event.

"To us, to me, also, certain fixed conventional limits are the basis of all happiness. To offend them is to be unhappy; to ignore them would mean destruction to our peace of mind and self-respect. And, though I do admire you and respect you for what you are, it is only just to you to say that we could never reconcile ourselves to those modern social conditions which you so charmingly represent, and which are embodied in you with such convincing dignity.

"Dear Miss West, have I pained you? Have I offended you in return for all your courtesy to me? I

333

hope not. I felt that I owed you this. Please accept it as a tribute and as a sorrowful acquiescence in conditions which an old-fashioned family are unable to change.

"Very sincerely yours,
"LILLY COLLIS."

She lay for a while, thinking, the sheets of the letter lying loose on the bed. It seemed to require no answer. Nor had Mrs. Collis, apparently, any fear that Valerie would ever inform Louis Neville of what had occurred between his sister and herself.

Still, to Valerie, an unanswered letter was like a civil observation ignored.

She wrote that evening to Lily:

"DEAR MRS. COLLIS: In acknowledging your letter of yesterday I beg to assure you that I understand the inadvisability of my marrying your brother, and that I have no idea of doing it, and that, through me, he shall never know of your letters or of your visit to me in his behalf.

"With many thanks for your kindly expressions of good-will toward me, I am

"Very truly yours,
"VALERIE WEST."

She had been too tired to call at Querida's studio, too tired even to take tea at the Plaza with Neville.

Rita came in, silent and out of spirits, and replied in monosyllables to Valerie's inquiries.

It finally transpired that Sam Ogilvy and Harry Annan had been tormenting John Burleson after their

again? You say to me, here's a man beginning to care for a girl who has been unwise enough before she knew him to let herself believe she cared enough for another man to become his mistress. Is that it, Rita?"

"Y-yes."

"Very well. What do you wish to ask me?"

"I wish to ask you what that girl should do."

"Do? Nothing. What is there for her to do?"

"Ought she to let that man care for her?"

"Has he ever made the same mistake she has?"

"I—don't think so."

"Are you sure?"

"Almost."

"Well, then, I'd tell him."

Rita lay silent, gazing into space, her blond hair clustering around the pretty oval of her face.

Valerie waited for a few moments, then resumed her reading, glancing inquiringly at intervals over the top of her book at Rita, who seemed disinclined for further conversation.

After a long silence she sat up abruptly on the sofa and looked at Valerie.

"You asked me who was the first man for whom I posed. I'll tell you if you wish to know. It was Penrhyn Cardemon! . . . And I was eighteen years old."

Valerie dropped her book in astonishment.

"Penrhyn Cardemon!" she repeated. "Why, he isn't an artist!"

"He has a studio."

"Where?"

"On Fifth Avenue."

"What does he do there?"

"Deviltry."

Rita looked up from the burnished disorder of her hair:

"I have been in love with him for three years," she said, "and you are the only person in the world except myself who knows it."

Valerie rose and walked over to Rita and seated herself beside her. Then she put one arm around her; and Rita bit her lip and stared at space, swinging her slender foot.

"You poor dear," said Valerie. Rita's bare foot hung inert; the silken slipper dropped from it to the floor; and then her head fell, sideways, resting on Valerie's shoulder, showering her body with its tangled gold.

Valerie said, thoughtfully: "Girls don't seem to have a very good chance. . . . I had no idea about Cardemon—that he was that kind of a man. A girl never knows. Men can be so attractive and so nice. . . . And so many of them are merciless. . . . I suppose you thought you loved him."

"Y-yes."

"We all think that, I suppose," said Valerie, thoughtfully.

"Other girls have thought it of Penrhyn Cardemon."

"Other *girls ?*"

"Yes."

Valerie's face expressed bewilderment.

"I didn't know that there were really such men."

Rita closed her disillusioned eyes.

"Plenty," she said wearily.

"I don't care to believe that."

"You may believe it, Valerie. Men are almost

" You? " inquired Annan wearily.

" Valerie West."

" What in God's name has that bunch taken her up for? "

For the last few weeks Valerie's telephone had rung intermittently summoning her to conversation with Mrs. Hind-Willet.

At first the amiable interest displayed by Mrs. Hind-Willet puzzled Valerie until one day, returning to her rooms for luncheon, she found the Countess d'Enver's brougham standing in front of the house and that discreetly perfumed lady about to descend.

" How do you do? " said Valerie, stopping on the sidewalk and offering her hand with a frank smile.

" I came to call on you," said the over-dressed little countess; " may I? "

" It is very kind of you. Will you come upstairs? There is no elevator."

The pretty bejewelled countess arrived in the living room out of breath, and seated herself, flushed, speechless, overcome, her little white gloved hand clutching her breast.

Valerie, accustomed to the climb, was in nowise distressed; and went serenely about her business while the countess was recovering.

" I am going to prepare luncheon; may I hope you will remain and share it with me? " she asked.

The countess nodded, slowly recovering her breath and glancing curiously around the room.

" You see I have only an hour between poses," observed Valerie, moving swiftly from cupboard to kitchenette, " so luncheon is always rather simple. Miss

Tevis, with whom I live, never lunches here, so I take
what there is left from breakfast."

A little later they were seated at a small table together, sipping chocolate. There was cold meat, a

The Countess d'Enver.

light salad, and fruit. The conversation was as haphazard and casual as the luncheon, until the pretty
countess lighted a cigarette and tasted her tiny glass
of Port—the latter a gift from Querida.

She leaned back among the cushions, dropping one knee over the other and tossing away her cigarette. And her little suede shoe swung nervously to and fro.

" You're the first girl I've seen in New York who, I believe, really doesn't care what I am—and I don't care what she is. Shall we be friends? I'm lonely."

Valérie looked at her, diffidently:

" I haven't had very much experience in friendship —except with Rita Tevis," she said.

" Will you let me take you to drive sometimes? "

" I'd love to, only you see I am in business."

" Of course I mean after hours.":

" Thank you. . . . But I usually am expected—to tea—and dinner——"

Hélène lay back among the cushions, looking at her.

" Haven't you any time at all for me? " she asked, wistfully.

Valerie was thinking of Neville: " Not—very—much I am afraid——"

" Can't you spare me an hour now and then? "

" Y-yes; I'll try."

There was a silence. The mantel clock struck, and Valerie glanced up. Hélène d'Enver rose, stood still a moment, then stepped forward and took both of Valerie's hands:

" Can't we be friends? I do need one; and I like you so much. You've the eyes that make a woman easy. There are none like yours in New York."

Valerie laughed, uncertainly.

" Your friends wouldn't care for me," she said. " I don't believe there is any real place at all for me in this city except among the few men and women I already know."

"Won't you include me among the number? There is a place for you in my heart."

Touched and surprised, the girl stood looking at the older woman in silence.

"May I drive you to your destination?" asked Hélène gently.

"You are very kind. . . . It is Mr. Burleson's studio—if it won't take you too far out of your way."

By the end of March Valerie had driven with the Countess d'Enver once or twice; and once or twice had been to see her, and had met, in her apartment, men and women who were inclined to make a fuss over her—men like Carrillo and Dennison, and women like Mrs. Hind-Willet and Mrs. Atherstane. It was her unconventional profession that interested them.

To Neville, recounting her experiences, she said with a patient little smile:

"It's rather nice to be liked and to have some kind of a place among people who live in this city. Nobody seems to mind my being a model. Perhaps they *have* taken merely a passing fancy to me and are exhibiting me to each other as a wild thing just captured and being trained—" She laughed—"but they do it so pleasantly that I don't mind. . . . And anyway, the Countess d'Enver is genuine; I am sure of that."

"A genuine countess?"

"A genuine woman, sincere, lovable, and kind—I am becoming very fond of her. . . . Do you mind my abandoning you for an afternoon now and then? Because it *is* nice to have as a friend a woman older and more experienced."

351

" Does that mean you're going off with her this afternoon? "

" I *was* going. But I won't if you feel that I'm deserting you."

He laid aside his palette and went over to where she was standing.

" You darling," he said, " go and drive in the Park with your funny little friend."

" She was going to take me to the Plaza for tea. There are to be some very nice women there who are interested in the New Idea Home." She added, shyly, " I have subscribed ten dollars."

He kissed her, lightly, humorously. " And what, sweetheart, may the New Idea Home be? "

" Oh, it's an idea of Mrs. Hind-Willet's about caring for wayward girls. Mrs. Willet thinks that it is cruel and silly to send them into virtual imprisonment, to punish them and watch them and confront them at every turn with threats and the merciless routine of discipline. She thinks that the thing to do is to give them a chance for sensible and normal happiness; not to segregate them one side of a dead line; not to treat them like criminals to be watched and doubted and suspected."

She linked her arms around his neck, interested, earnest, sure of his sympathy and approval:

" We want to build a school in the country—two schools, one for girls who have misbehaved, one for youths who are similarly delinquent. And, during recreation, we mean to let them meet in a natural manner—play games together, dance, mingle out of doors in a wholesome and innocent way—of course, under necessary and sympathetic supervision—and learn a healthy consideration and respect for one another which the squalid, crowded, irresponsible conditions of their former street life in the slums and tenements made utterly impossible."

He looked into the pretty, eager face with its honest, beautiful eyes and sensitive mouth—and touched his lips to her hair.

" It sounds fine, sweetheart," he said: " and I won't be lonely if you go to the Plaza and settle the affairs of this topsy-turvy world. . . . Do you love me? "

" Louis! Can you ask? "

" I do ask."

She smiled, faintly; then her young face grew serious, and a hint of passion darkened her eyes as her arms tightened around his neck and her lips met his.

" All I care for in the world, or out of it, is you, Louis. If I find pleasure in anything it is because of you; if I take a little pride in having people like me, it is only for your sake—for the sake of the pride you may feel in having others find me agreeable and desirable. I wish it were possible that your own world could find me agreeable and desirable—for your sake, my darling, more than for mine. But it never will—never could. There is a wall around your world which I can never scale. And it does not make me unhappy—I only wish you to know that I want to be what you would have me—and if I can't be all that you might wish, I love and adore you none the less—am none the less willing to give you all there is to me—all there is to a girl named Valerie West who finds this life a happy one because you have made it so for her."

She continued to see Hélène d'Enver, poured tea sometimes at the Five-Minute-Club, listened to the consultations over the New Idea Home, and met a great many people of all kinds, fashionable women with a passion for the bizarre and unconventional, women of gentle breeding and no social pretence, who worked to support themselves; idle women, ambitious women, restless women; but the majority formed part of the floating circles domiciled in apartments and at the great hotels—people who wintered in New York and were a part of its social and civic life to that extent, but whose duties and responsibilities for the metropolitan welfare were self-imposed, and neither hereditary nor constant.

As all circles in New York have, at certain irregular periods, accidental points of temporary contact, Valerie now and then met people whom she was scarcely even likely to see again. And it was at a New Idea Home conference, scheduled for five o'clock in the red parlour of the ladies' waiting room in the great Hotel Imperator, that Valerie, arriving early as delegated substitute for Mrs. Hind-Willet, found herself among a small group of beautifully gowned strangers—the sort of women whom she had never before met in this way.

They all knew each other; others who arrived seemed to recognise with more or less intimacy everybody in the room excepting herself.

She was sitting apart by the crimson-curtained windows, perfectly self-possessed and rather interested in watching the arrivals of women whose names, as she caught them, suggested social positions which were vaguely familiar to her, when an exceedingly pretty girl detached herself from the increasing group and came across to where Valerie was sitting alone.

354

" 'May I sit here with you until she arrives? I am Stephanie Swift.' "

"I was wondering whether you had met any of the
new committee," she said pleasantly.

"I *had* expected to meet the Countess d'Enver here,"
said Valerie, smiling.

The girl's expression altered slightly, but she
nodded amiably; "May I sit here with you until she
arrives? I am Stephanie Swift."

Valerie said: "It is very amiable of you. I am
Valerie West."

Stephanie remained perfectly still for a moment;
then, conscious that she was staring, calmly averted her
gaze while the slow fire died out in her cheeks. And in
a moment she had decided:

"I have heard so pleasantly about you through

Mrs. Collis," she said with perfect composure. "You remember her, I think."

Valerie, startled, lifted her brown eyes. Then very quietly:

"Mrs. Collis is very kind. I remember her distinctly."

"Mrs. Collis retains the most agreeable memories of meeting you. . . . I—" she looked at Valerie, curiously—"I have heard from others how charming and clever you are—from Mr. Ogilvy?—and Mr. Annan?"

"They are my friends," said Valerie briefly.

"And Mr. Querida, and Mr. Burleson, and—Mr. Neville."

"They are my friends," repeated Valerie. . . . After a second she added: "They also employ me."

Stephanie looked away: "Your profession must be most interesting, Miss West."

"Yes."

"But—exacting."

"Very."

Neither made any further effort. A moment later, however, Hélène d'Enver came in. She knew some of the women very slightly, none intimately; and, catching sight of Valerie, she came across the room with a quick smile of recognition:

"I'm dreadfully late, dear—how do you do, Miss Swift "—to Stephanie, who had risen. And to Valerie: "Mr. Ogilvy came just as I had my furs on—and you know how casually a man takes his leave when you're in a tearing hurry!"

She laughed and took Valerie's gloved hands in her own; and Stephanie, who had been looking at the lat-

"I knew, of course, that she was from Massachusetts," said John, "because she speaks English properly. So I asked her where she was born and she told me. . . . My grandfather knew hers."

"Isn't it—curious," mused the girl.

"What's curious?"

"Your meeting this way—as sculptor and model."

"Rita is a very fine girl," he said. "Would you mind handing me my pipe? No, don't. I forgot that Rita won't let me. You see my chest is rather uncomfortable."

He glanced at the clock, leaned over and gulped down some medicine, then placidly folding his hands, lay back:

"How's Kelly?"

"I haven't seen him to-day, John."

"Well, he ought to be here very soon. He can take you and Rita to dinner."

"I'm so sorry you can't come."

"So am I."

Valerie laid a cool hand on his face; he seemed slightly feverish. Rita came in at that moment, smiled at Valerie, and went straight to Burleson's couch:

"Have you taken your medicine?"

"Certainly."

She glanced at the bottles. "Men are so horridly untruthful," she remarked to Valerie; "and this great, lumbering six-footer hasn't the sense of a baby——"

"I have, too!" roared John, indignantly; and Valerie laughed but Rita scarcely smiled.

"He's always working in a puddle of wet clay and he's always having colds and coughing, and there's always more or less fever," she said, looking down at the huge young fellow. "I know that he ought to give up his work and go away for a while——"

"Where?" demanded Burleson indignantly.

"Oh, somewhere—where there's plenty of—air. Like Arizona, and Colorado.

"Do you think there's anything the matter with my lungs?" he roared.

"No!—you perfect idiot!" said Rita, seating herself; "and if you shout that way at me again I'll go to dinner with Kelly and Valerie and leave you here alone. I will not permit you to be uncivil, John. Please remember it."

Neville arrived in excellent spirits, greeted everybody, and stood beside Valerie, carelessly touching the tip of his fingers to hers where they hung at her side.

"What's the matter with *you*, John? Rita, isn't he coming? I've a taxi outside ruining me."

"John has a bad cold and doesn't care to go——"

"Yes, I do!" growled John.

"And he doesn't care to risk contracting pneumonia," continued Rita icily, "and he isn't going, anyway. And if he behaves like a man instead of an overgrown baby, I have promised to stay and dine with him here. Otherwise I'll go with you."

"Sure. You'd better stay indoors, John. You ought to buck up and get rid of that cold. It's been hanging on all winter."

Burleson rumbled and grumbled and shot a mutinous glance at Rita, who paid it no attention.

"Order us a nice dinner at the Plaza, Kelly—if you don't mind," she said cheerfully, going with them to the door. She added under her breath: "I wish he'd

361

see a doctor, but the idea enrages him. I don't see why he has such a cold all the time—and such flushed cheeks—" Her voice quivered and she checked herself abruptly.

"Suppose I ring up Dr. Colbert on my own hook?" whispered Neville.

"Would you?"

"Certainly. And you can tell John that I did it on my own responsibility."

Neville and Valerie went away together, and Rita returned to the studio. Burleson was reading again, and scowling; and he scarcely noticed her. She seated herself by the fire and looked into the big bare studio beyond where the electric light threw strange shadows over shrouded shapes of wet clay and blocks of marble in the rough or partly hewn into rough semblance of human figures.

It was a damp place at best; there were always wet sponges, wet cloths, pails of water, masses of moist clay about. Her blue eyes wandered over it with something approaching fear—almost the fear of hatred.

"John," she said, "why won't you go to a dry climate for a few months and get rid of your cold?"

"Do you mean Arizona?"

"Or some similar place: yes."

"Well, how am I to do any work out there? I've got commissions on hand. Where am I going to find any place to work out in Arizona?"

"Build a shanty."

"That's all very well, but there are no models to be had out there."

"Why don't you do some Indians?"

"Because," said John wrathfully, "I haven't any

commissions that call for Indians. I've two angels, a nymph and a Diana to do; and I can't do them unless I have a female model, can I? "

After a silence Rita said carelessly:

" I'll go with you if you like."

" You! Out there! "

" I said so."

" To Arizona! You wouldn't stand for it! "

" John Burleson! " she said impatiently, " I've told you once that I'd go with you if you need a model! Don't you suppose I know what I am saying? "

He lay placidly staring at her, the heavy book open across his chest. Presently he coughed and Rita sprang up and removed the book.

" You'd go with me to Arizona," he repeated, as though to himself—"just to pose for me. . . . That's very kind of you, Rita. It's thoroughly nice of you. But you couldn't stand it. You'd find it too cruelly stupid out there alone—entirely isolated in some funny town. I couldn't ask it of you——"

" You haven't. I've asked it—of you."

But he only began to grumble and fret again, thrashing about restlessly on the lounge; and the tall young girl watched him out of lowered eyes, silent, serious, the lamplight edging her hair with a halo of ruddy gold.

The month sped away very swiftly for Valerie. Her companionship with Rita, her new friendship for Hélène d'Enver, her work, filled all the little moments not occupied with Neville. It had been a happy, exciting winter; and now, with the first days of spring, an excitement and a happiness so strange that it even

day. They're seen together everywhere except where Louis really belongs."

"It looks to me," said Gordon mildly, "as though he were really in love with her."

"Gordon! How *can* you say such a thing in such a sympathetic tone!"

"Why—aren't you sorry for them?"

"I'm sorry for Louis—and perfectly disgusted. I *was* sorry for her; an excess of sentimentality. But she hasn't kept her word to me."

"Did she promise not to gad about with him?"

"That was the spirit of the compact; she agreed not to marry him."

"Sometimes they—don't marry," observed Gordon, twirling his thumbs.

Lily looked up quickly; then flushed slightly.

"What do you mean, Gordon?"

"Nothing specific; anything in general."

"You mean to hint that—that Louis—Louis Neville could be—permit himself to be so common—so unutterably low——"

"Better men have taken the half-loaf."

"Gordon!" she exclaimed, scarlet with amazement and indignation.

"Personally," he said, unperturbed, "I haven't much sympathy with such affairs. If a man can't marry a girl he ought to leave her alone; that's my idea of the game. But men play it in a variety of ways. Personally, I'd as soon plug a loaded shot-gun with mud and then fire it, as block a man who wants to marry."

"I *did* block it!" said Lily with angry decision; "and I am glad I did."

"Look out for the explosion then," he said philosophically, and strolled off to see to the setting out of some young hemlocks, headed in the year previous.

Lily Collis was deeply disturbed—more deeply than her pride and her sophistication cared to admit. She strove to believe that such a horror as her husband had hinted at so coolly could never happen to a Neville; she rejected it with anger, with fear, with a proud and dainty fastidiousness that ought to have calmed and reassured her. It did not.

Once or twice she reverted to the subject, haughtily; but Gordon merely shrugged:

"You can't teach a man of twenty-eight when, where, and how to fall in love," he said. "And it's all the more hopeless when the girl possesses the qualities which you once told me this girl possesses."

Lily bit her lip, angry and disconcerted, but utterly unable to refute him or find anything in her memory of Valerie to criticise and condemn, except the intimacy with her brother which had continued and which, she had supposed, would cease on Valerie's promise to her.

"It's very horrid of her to go about with him under the circumstances—knowing she can't marry him if she keeps her word," said Lily.

"Why? Stephanie goes about with him."

"Do you think it is good taste to compare those two people?"

"Why not. From what you told me I gather that Valerie West is as innocent and upright a woman as Stephanie—and as proudly capable of self-sacrifice as any woman who ever loved."

"Gordon," she said, exasperated, "do you actually wish to see my brother marry a common model?"

"*Is* she common?   I thought you said——"

"You—you annoy me," said Lily; and began to cry.

Stephanie, coming into the nursery that afternoon, found Lily watching the sleeping children and knitting a tiny sweater.   Mrs. Collis was pale, but her eyes were still red.

"Where have you been, Stephanie?"

"Helping Gordon set hemlocks."

"Where is Louis?"

The girl did not appear to hear the question.

"I thought I heard him telephoning a few minutes ago," added Lily.   "Look over the banisters, dear, and see if he's still there."

"He is," said Stephanie, not stirring.

"Telephoning all this time?   Is he talking to somebody in town?"

"I believe so."

Lily suddenly looked up.   Stephanie was quietly examining some recently laundered clothing for the children.

"To whom is Louis talking; do you happen to know?" asked Lily abruptly.

Stephanie's serious gaze encountered hers.

"Does that concern us, Lily?"

After a while, as Mrs. Collis sat in silence working her ivory needles, a tear or two fell silently upon the little white wool garment on her lap.

And presently Stephanie went over and touched her forehead with gentle lips; but Lily did not look up—could not—and her fingers and ivory needles flew the faster.

"Do you know," said Stephanie in a low voice,

" that she is a modest, well-bred, and very beautiful girl? "

" What! " exclaimed Lily, staring at her in grief and amazement. " Of whom are you speaking, Stephanie? "

" Of Valerie West, dear."

" W-what do you know about her? "

" I have met her."

" *You!* "

" Yes. She came, with that rather common countess, as substitute delegate for Mrs. Hind-Willet, to a New Idea meeting. I spoke to her, seeing she was alone and seemed to know nobody; I had no suspicion of who she was until she told me."

" Mrs. Hind-Willet is a busybody! " said Lily, furious. " Let her fill her own drawing-room with freaks if it pleases her, but she has no right to send them abroad among self-respecting people who are too unsuspicious to protect themselves! "

Stephanie said: " Until one has seen and spoken with Valerie West one can scarcely understand how a man like your brother could care so much for her——"

" How do you know Louis cares for her? "

" He told me."

Lily looked into the frank, gray eyes in horror unutterable. The crash had come. The last feeble hope that her brother might come to his senses and marry this girl was ended forever.

" How—could he! " she stammered, outraged. " How could he tell—tell *you*——"

" Because he and I are old and close friends, Lily. . . . And will remain so, God willing."

marriage—that drove Lily Collis to write once more to Valerie West:

"DEAR MISS WEST: It is not that I have any disposition to doubt your word to me, but, in view of the assurance you have given me, do you consider it wise to permit my brother's rather conspicuous attentions to you?

"Permit me, my dear Miss West, as an older woman with wider experience which years must bring, to suggest that it is due to yourself to curtail an intimacy which the world—of course mistakenly in your case—views always uncharitably.

"No man—and I include my brother as severely as I do any man—has a right to let the world form any misconception as to his intentions toward any woman. If he does he is either ignorant or selfish and ruthless; and it behooves a girl to protect her own reputation.

"I write this in all faith and kindliness for your sake as well as for his. But a man outlives such things; a woman never. And, for the sake of your own future I beg you to consider this matter and I trust that you may not misconstrue the motive which has given me the courage to write you what has caused me deepest concern.

"Very sincerely yours,

"LILY COLLIS."

To which Valerie replied:

"MY DEAR MRS. COLLIS: I have to thank you for your excellent intentions in writing me. But with all deference to your wider experience I am afraid that I must remain the judge of my own conduct. Pray, believe that, in proportion to your sincerity, I am grateful to you; and that I should never dream of being discourteous to Mr. Neville's sister if I venture to suggest to her that liberty of conscience is a fundamental scarcely susceptible of argument or discussion.

"I assume that you would not care to have Mr. Neville know of this correspondence, and for that reason I am returning to you your letter so that you may be assured of its ultimate destruction.

"Very truly yours,
"VALERIE WEST."

Which letter and its reply made Valerie deeply unhappy; and she wrote Neville a little note saying that she had gone to the country with Hélène d'Enver for a few days' rest.

The countess had taken a house among the hills at Estwich; and as chance would have it, about eight miles from Ashuelyn and Penrhyn Cardemon's great establishment, El Naúar.

Later Valerie was surprised and disturbed to learn of the proximity of Neville's family, fearing that if Mrs. Collis heard of her in the neighbourhood she might misunderstand.

But there was only scant and rough communication between Ashuelyn and Estwich; the road was a wretched hill-path passable only by buck-boards; Westwich was the nearest town to Ashuelyn and El Naúar and the city of Dartford, the county seat most convenient to Estwich.

Spring was early; the Estwich hills bloomed in May; and Hélène d'Enver moved her numerous household from the huge Castilione Apartment House to Estwich and settled down for a summer of mental and physical recuperation.

Valerie, writing to Neville the first week in May, said:

"Louis, the country here is divine. I thought the shaggy, unkempt hills of Delaware County were heavenly—and they *were* when you came and made them so —but this rich, green, well-ordered country with its hills and woods and meadows of emerald—its calm river, its lovely little brooks, its gardens, hedges, farms, is to me the most wonderful land I ever looked upon.

"Hélène has a pretty house, white with green blinds and verandas, and the loveliest lawns you ever saw— unless the English lawns are lovelier.

"To my city-wearied eyes the region is celestial in its horizon-wide quiet. Only the ripple of water in leafy ravines—only the music of birds breaks the silence that is so welcome, so blessed.

"To-day Hélène and I picked strawberries for breakfast, then filled the house with great fragrant peonies, some of which are the colour of Brides' roses, some of water-lilies.

"I'm quite mad with delight; I love the farm with its ducks and hens and pigeons; I adore the cattle in the meadow. They are fragrant. Hélène laughs at me because I follow the cows about, sniffing luxuriously. They smell like the clover they chew.

"Louis, dear, I have decided to remain a week here, if you don't mind. I'm a little tired, I think. John Burleson, poor boy, does not need me. I'm terribly

worried about him. Rita writes that there is no danger of pneumonia, but that Dr. Colbert is making a
careful examination. I hope it is not lung trouble. It
would be too tragic. He is only twenty-seven. Still,
they cure such things now, don't they? Rita is hoping
he will go to Arizona, and has offered to go with him
as his model. That means—if she does go—that she'll
nurse him and take care of him. She is devoted to
him. What a generous girl she is!

"Dear, if you don't need me, or are not too lonely
without seeing me come fluttering into your studio
every evening at tea-time, I would really like to remain
here a few days longer. I have arranged business so
that I can stay if it is agreeable to you. Tell me
exactly how you feel about it and I will do exactly
as you wish—which, please God—I shall always do
while life lasts.

"Sam came up over Sunday, lugging Harry Annan
and a bulldog—a present for Hélène. Sam is *so* sentimental about Hélène!

"And he's so droll about it. But I've seen him that
way before; haven't you? And Hélène, bless her heart,
lets him make eyes at her and just laughs in that
happy, wholesome way of hers.

"She's a perfect dear, Louis; so sweet and kind to
me, so unaffected, so genuine, so humorous about herself and her funny title. She told me that she would
gladly shed it if she were not obliged to shed her legacy
with it. I don't blame her. What an awful title—
when you translate it!

"Sam is temporarily laid up. He attempted to
milk a cow and she kicked him; and he's lying in a hammock and Hélène is reading to him, while Harry paints

in the magic of this air and sunshine I have watched the reincarnation of myself. I swim, I row, I am learning to sit a horse; I play tennis—*and* I flirt, Monsieur—shamelessly, with Sam and Harry. Do you object——

"We had such a delightful time—a week-end party, perfectly informal and crazy; Mrs. Hind-Willet—who is such a funny woman, considering the position she might occupy in society—and José Querida—just six of us, until—and this I'm afraid you may not like—Mrs. Hind-Willet telephoned Penrhyn Cardemon to come over.

"You know, Louis, he *seems* a gentleman, though it is perfectly certain that he isn't. I hate and despise him; and have been barely civil to him. But in a small company one has to endure such things with outward equanimity; and I am sure that nobody suspects my contempt for him and that my dislike has not caused one awkward moment."

She wrote again:

"I beg of you not to suggest to your sister that she call on me. Try to be reasonable, dear. Mrs. Collis does not desire to know me. Why should she? Why should you wish to have me meet her? If you have any vague ideas that my meeting her might in any possible way alter a situation which must always exist between your family and myself, you are utterly mistaken, dearest.

"And my acquaintance with Miss Swift is so slight—I never saw her but once, and then only for a moment!—that it would be only painful and embarrassing

375

something to her. And men don't seem to understand that."

"Mrs. Hind-Willet departs to-morrow. Sam and Harry go to Ashuelyn; Mr. Cardemon to his rural palace, I devoutly trust; which will leave José to Hélène and me; and he's equal to it.

"How long may I stay, dear? I am having a heavenly time—which is odd because heaven is in New York just now."

Another letter in answer to one of his was briefer:

"MY DARLING:

"Certainly you must go to Ashuelyn if your father and mother wish it. They are old, dear; and it is a heartless thing to thwart the old.

"Don't think of attempting to come over here to see me. The chances are that your family would hear of it and it would only pain them. Any happiness that you and I are ever to have must not be gained at any expense to them.

"So keep your distance, Monsieur; make your parents and your sister happy for the few days you are to be there; and on Thursday I will meet you on the 9.30 train and we will go back to town together.

"I am going anyway, for two reasons; I have been away from you entirely too long, and—the First of June is very, very near.

"I love you with all my heart, Louis.
                    "VALERIE WEST."

13

aloof, wrapped in his memories, like one who listens to phantoms in a dream praising perfection.

Lying back in his chair before his canvas, he thought of her often—of odd little details concerning their daily life—details almost trivial—gestures, a glance, a laugh—recollections which surprised him with the very charm of their insignificance.

He remembered that he had never known her to be ungenerous—had never detected in her a wilfully selfish motive. In his life he had never before believed in a character so utterly unshackled by thought of self.

He remembered that he had never known her to fail in sympathy for any living thing; had never detected in her an indifference to either the happiness or the sorrow of others. In his life he had never before believed that the command to love one's neighbour had in it anything more significant than the beauty of an immortal theory. He believed it now because, in her; he had seen it in effortless practice. He was even beginning to understand how it might be possible for him to follow where she led—as she, unconsciously, was a follower of a precept given to lead the world through eternities.

Leaning on the closed piano, thinking of her in the still, sunny afternoons, faintly in his ears her voice seemed to sound; and he remembered her choice of ballads:—

> —"For even the blind distinguisheth
>   The king with his robe and crown;
> But only the humble eye of faith
> Beholdeth Jesus of Nazareth
>   In the beggar's tattered gown.

381

and sits on fences talking to various Rubes. Stephanie floats about like a well-fed angel, with a fox-terrier, and makes a monkey of me at tennis whenever I'm lunatic enough to let her, and generally dispenses sweetness, wholesomeness, and light upon a worthy household. I wouldn't mind marrying that girl," he added casually. "What do you think?"

Neville laughed: "Why don't you? She's the nicest girl I ever knew—almost."

"I'd ask her to marry me," said Cameron facetiously; "only I'm afraid such a dazzling prospect would turn her head and completely spoil her."

He spoke gaily and laughed loudly—almost boisterously. Neville glanced at him with a feeling that Cameron was slightly overdoing it—rather forcing the mirth without any particular reason.

After a moment he said: "Sandy, you don't have to be a clown if you don't want to be, you know."

"Can't help it," said Cameron, reddening; "everybody expects it now. When Ogilvy was here we played in a double ring to crowded houses. Every seat on the veranda was taken; we turned 'em away, my boy. *What* was it you started to say about Stephanie?"

"I didn't start to say anything about Stephanie."

"Oh, I thought you were going to "—his voice died into an uncertain grumble. Neville glanced at him again, thoughtfully.

"You know, Sandy," he said, "that there's another side to you—which, for some occult reason you seem to hide—even to be ashamed of."

"Sure I'm ashamed to be a broker with all you highbrows lining out homers for the girls while I have to sit on the bleachers and score 'em up. If I try to make a hit with the ladies it's a bingle; and it's the bench and the bush-league for muh——"

"You great, overgrown kid! It's a pity people can't see you down town. Everybody knows you're the cleverest thing south of Broad and Wall. Look at all the boards, all the committees, all the directorates you're mixed up with! Look at all the time you give freely to others—look at all your charities, all your civic activities, all——"

"All the hell I raise!" said Cameron, very red. "Don't forget that, Louis!"

"You never did—that's the wonder and the eternal decency of you, Cameron. You're a good citizen and a good man, and you do more for the world than we painters ever could do! That's the real truth of it; and why you so persistently try to represent yourself as a commonplace something else is beyond me—and probably beyond Stephanie Swift," he added carelessly.

They whizzed along in silence for some time, and it was only when Ashuelyn was in sight that Cameron suddenly turned and held out his hand:

"Thank you, Louis; you've said some very kind things."

Neville shrugged: "I hear you are financing that New Idea Home. I tell you that's a fine conception."

But Cameron only looked modest. At heart he was a very shy man and he deprecated any idea that he was doing anything unusual in giving most of his time to affairs that paid dividends only in happiness and in the consciousness of moral obligation fulfilled.

The household was occupying the pergola as they arrived and sprang out upon the clipped lawn.

Neville kissed his mother tenderly, shook hands cor-

The unmounted imprint passed from hand to hand amid various comments.

"It is very beautiful, Louis," said his mother, with a smile of pride; and even as she spoke the smile faded and her sad eyes rested on him wistfully.

"Is it a sacred picture?" asked his father, examining it through his glasses without the slightest trace of interest.

"It is an Annunciation, isn't it?" inquired Lily, calmly. But her heart was failing her, for in the beauty of the exquisite, enraptured face, she saw what might have been the very soul of Valerie West.

His father, removing his spectacles, delivered himself of an opinion concerning mysticism, and betrayed an illogical tendency to drift toward the Concord School of Philosophy. However, there seemed to be insufficient incentive; he glanced coldly toward Cameron and resumed Herbert Spencer and his spectacles.

"Mother, don't you want to stroll on the lawn a bit?" he asked presently. "It looks very inviting to a city man's pavement-worn feet."

She drew her light wool shawl around her shoulders and took her tall son's arm.

For a long while they strolled in silence, passed idly through the garden where masses of peonies hung over the paths, and pansies, iris, and forget-me-nots made the place fragrant.

It was not until they came to the plank bridge where the meadow rivulet, under its beds of cress and mint, threaded a shining way toward the woods, that his mother said in a troubled voice:

"You are not happy, Louis."

"Why, mother—what an odd idea!"

like men who have known sorrow. . . . What sorrow
have you ever known, Louis?"

"None. No great one, mother. Perhaps, lately,
I have developed—recognised—become aware of the
sombre part of life—become sensitive to it—to unhappiness in others—and have cared more——"

"You speak like a man who has suffered."

"But I haven't, mother," he insisted. "Of course,
every painter worries. I did last winter—last winter—" He hesitated, conscious that last winter—
on the snowy threshold of the new year—sorrow and
pain and happiness and pity had, in an instant, assumed
for him a significance totally new.

"Mother," he said slowly, "if I have changed it is
only in a better understanding of the world and those
who live in it. I have cared very little about people;
I seem to have come to care more, lately. What they
did, what they thought, hoped, desired, endured, suffered, interested me little except as it concerned my
work. And somehow, since then, I am becoming interested in people for their own sakes. It's a—new sensation."

He smiled and laid his hand over hers:

"Do you know I never even appreciated what a
good man Alexander Cameron is until recently. Why,
mother, that man is one of the most generous, modest,
kind, charitable, unselfish fellows in the world!"

"His behaviour is sometimes a little extraordinary,"
said his mother—"isn't it?"

"Oh, that's all on the surface! He's full of boyish
spirits. He dearly loves a joke—but the greater part
of that interminable funny business is merely to mask
the modesty of a man whose particular perversity is a

fear that people might discover how kind and how clever he really is!"

They walked on in silence for a while, then his mother said:

"Mr. Querida was here. Is he a friend of yours?"

Neville hesitated: "I'll tell you, mother," he said, "I don't find Querida personally very congenial. But I have no doubt he's an exceedingly nice fellow. And he's far and away the best painter in America. . . . When did he go back to town?"

"Last week. I did not care for him."

"You and father seldom do care for new acquaintances," he rejoined, smiling. "Don't you think it is about time for you to emerge from your shells and make up your minds that a few people have been born since you retired?"

"People have been born in China, too, but that scarcely interests your father and me."

"Let it interest you, mother. You have no idea how amusing new people are. That's the way to keep young, too."

"It is a little too late for us to think of youth— or to think as youth thinks—even if it were desirable."

"It *is* desirable. Youth—which will be age to-morrow—may venture to draw a little consideration in advance——"

"My children interest me—and I give their youth my full consideration. But I can scarcely be expected to find any further vital interest in youth—and in the complexity of its modern views and ideas. You ask impossibilities of two very old people."

"I do not mean to. I ask only, then, that you and

"Not when you know her."

"Lily knows her and is bitterly opposed to her——"

"What!" he exclaimed, astounded. "You say that my sister knows Valerie West?"

"I—forgot," faltered his mother; "I ought not to have said anything."

"Where did Lily meet her?" he asked, bewildered.

"Don't ask me, Louis. I should not have spoken——"

"Yes, you should have! It is my affair; it concerns me—and it concerns Valerie—her future and mine—our happiness. Where did Lily meet her?"

"You must ask that of Lily. I cannot and will not discuss it. I will say only this: I have seen the —this Miss West. She is at present a guest at the villa of a—countess—of whom neither your father nor I ever before heard—and whom even Lily knows so slightly that she scarcely bows to her. And yesterday, while motoring, we met them driving on the Estwich road and your sister told us who they were."

After a moment he said slowly: "So you have actually seen the girl I am in love with?"

"I saw—Miss West."

"Can't you understand that I *am* in love with her?"

"Even if you are it is better for you to conquer your inclination——"

"Why?"

"Because all your life long you will regret such a marriage."

"Why?"

"Because nobody will care to receive a woman for

whom you can make no explanation—even if you are married to her."

He kept his patience.

" Will *you* receive her, mother? "

She closed her eyes, drew a quick, painful breath: " My son's wife—whoever she may be—will meet with no discourtesy under my roof."

" Is that the best you can offer us? "

" Louis! Louis!—if it lay only with me—I would do what you wished—even this—if it made you happy——"

He took her in his arms and kissed her in silence.

" You don't understand," she said,—" it is not I— it is the family—our entire little world against her. It would be only an eternal, hopeless, heart-breaking struggle for you, and for her;—pain for you—deep pain and resentment and bitterness for those who did not—perhaps could not—take your views of——"

" I don't care, mother, as long as you and father and Lily stand by her. And Valerie won't marry me unless you do. I didn't tell you that, but it is the truth. And I'm fighting very hard to win her—harder than you know—or will ever know. Don't embitter me; don't let me give up. Because, if I do, it means desperation—and things which you never could understand. . . . And I want you to talk to father. Will you? And to Lily, too. Its fairer to warn her that I have learned of her meeting Valerie. Then I'll talk to them both and see what can be done. . . . And, mother, I am very happy and very grateful and very proud that you are going to stand by me—and by the loveliest girl in all the world."

That night Lily came to his room. Her eyes were red, but there was fire in them. She seated herself and surveyed her brother with ominous self-possession.

"Well, Lily," he said pleasantly, prepared to keep his temper at all hazards.

"Well, Louis, I understand from mother that you have some questions to ask me."

"No questions, little sister; only your sympathetic attention while I tell you how matters stand with me."

"You require too much!" she said shortly.

"If I ask for your sympathy?"

"Not if you ask it for yourself, Louis. But if you include that——"

"Please, dear!" he interrupted, checking her with a slight gesture—for an instant only; then she went on in a determined voice:

"Louis, I might as well tell you at once that I have no sympathy for her. I wrote to her, out of sheer kindness, for her own good—and she replied so insolently that—that I am not yet perfectly recovered——"

"What did you write?"

Mrs. Collis remained disdainfully silent, but her eyes sparkled.

"Won't you tell me," he asked, patiently, "what it was you wrote to Valerie West?"

"Yes, I'll tell you if you insist on knowing!— even if you do misconstrue it! I wrote to her— for her own sake—and to avoid ill-natured comment,— suggesting that she be seen less frequently with you in public. I wrote as nicely, as kindly, as delicately as I knew how. And her reply was a practical request that I mind my business! . . . Which was vulgar and outrageous, considering that she had given me her prom-

Lily was breathing fast; her eyes narrowed unpleasantly.

He managed to master his astonishment and anger; but it was a heavy draught on his reserve of self-discipline, good temper, and common sense to pass over this thing that had been done to him and to concentrate himself upon the main issue. When he was able to speak again, calmly and without resentment, he said:

"The first thing for us to do, as a family, is to eliminate all personal bitterness from this discussion. There must be no question of our affection for one another; no question but what we wish to do the best by each other. I accept that as granted. If you took the step which you did take it was because you really believed it necessary for my happiness——"

"I still believe it!" she insisted; and her lips became a thin, hard line.

"Then we won't discuss it. But I want to ask you one thing; have you talked with mother about it?"

"Yes—naturally."

"Has she told you all that I told her this afternoon?"

"I suppose so. It does not alter my opinion one particle," she replied, her pretty head obstinately lowered.

He said: "Valerie West will not marry me if my family continues hostile to her."

Lily slowly lifted her eyes:

"Then will you tell me why she permits herself to be seen so constantly with you? If she is not going to marry you what *is* she going to do? Does she care what people are saying about her?—and about you?"

"No decent people are likely to say anything un-as threatens—I mean—I mean—oh, Louis! Try to understand us and sympathise a little with us!"

His arms closed around her shoulders:

"Little sister, we both have the family temper—and beneath it, the family instinct for cohesion. If we are also selfish it is not individual but family selfishness. It is the family which has always said to the world, '*Noli me tangere!*' while we, individually, are really inclined to be kinder, more sympathetic, more curious about the neighbours outside our gate. Let it be so now. Once inside the family, what can harm Valerie?"

"Dearest, dearest brother," she murmured, "you talk like a foolish man. Women understand better. And if it is a part of your program that this girl is to be accepted by an old-fashioned society, now almost obsolete, but in which this family is merely a single superannuated unit, that program can never be carried out."

"I think you are mistaken," he said.

"I know I am not. It is inevitable that if you marry this girl she will be more or less ignored, isolated, humiliated, overlooked outside our own little family circle. Even in that limited mob which the newspapers call New York Society—in that modern, wealthy, hard-witted, over-jewelled, self-sufficient league which is yet too eternally uncertain of its own status to assume any authority or any responsibility for a stranger without credentials,—it would not be possible to make Valerie West acceptable in the slightest sense of the word. Because she is too well known; her beauty is celebrated; she has become famous. Her only chance there—or with us—would have been in her absolute anonymity. Then lies *might* have done the rest. But lying is now useless in regard to her."

" Perfectly," he said. " She would not permit it."

In his vacant gaze there was something changed—a fixedness born of a slow and hopeless enlightenment.

" If that is the case, there is no chance," he said thoughtfully. " I had not considered that aspect."

" I had."

He shook his head slightly, gazing through the window at the starry lustre overhead.

" I wouldn't care," he said, " if she would only marry me. If she'd do that I'd never bother anybody —nor embarrass the family——"

" Louis ! "

" I mean make any social demands on you. . . . And, as for the world—" He slowly shook his head again: " We could make our own friends and our own way—if she would only consent to do it. But she never will."

" Do you mean to say she will not marry you if you ask her? " began Lily incredulously.

" Absolutely."

" Why? "

" For your sakes—yours, and mother's, and father's—and for mine."

There was a long silence, then Lily said unsteadily:

" There—there seems to be a certain—nobility— about her. . . . It is a pity—a tragedy—that she is what she is! "

" It is a tragedy that the world is what it is," he said. " Good night."

His father sent for him in the morning; Louis found

him reading the *Tribune* in his room and sipping a
bowl of hot milk and toast.

"What have you been saying to your mother?" he

"'What have you been saying to your mother?' he asked."

asked, looking up through his gold-rimmed spectacles
and munching toast.

"Has she not told you, father?"

"Yes, she has. . . . I think you had better make a
trip around the world."

" That would not alter matters."

" I differ with you," observed his father, leisurely employing his napkin.

" There is no use considering it," said his son patiently.

" Then what do you propose to do? "

" There is nothing to do."

" By that somewhat indefinite expression I suppose that you intend to pursue a waiting policy? "

" A waiting policy? " His son laughed, mirthlessly. " What am I to wait for? If you all were kind to Valerie West she might, perhaps, consent to marry me. But it seems that even our own family circle has not sufficient authority to protect her from our friends' neglect and humiliation. . . .

" She warned me that it would be so, long ago. I did not believe it; I could not comprehend it. But, somehow, Lily has made me believe it. And so have you. I guess it must be true. And if that's all I have to offer my wife, it's not enough to compensate her for her loss of freedom and happiness and self-respect among those who really care for her."

" Do you give me to understand that you renounce all intentions of marrying this girl? " asked his father, breaking more toast into his bowl of milk.

" Yes," said his son, listlessly.

" Thank God! " said his father; " come here, my son."

They shook hands; the son's lifeless arm fell to his side and he stood looking at the floor in silence. The father took a spoonful of hot milk with satisfaction, and, after the younger man had left the room, he resumed his newspaper. He was particularly interested in the " Sunshine Column," which dispensed sweetness and light under a poetic caption too beautiful to be true in a coldly humorous world.

That afternoon Gordon Collis said abruptly to Neville:

" You look like the devil, Louis."

" Do I? "

" You certainly do." And, in a lower voice: " I guess I've heard what's the matter. Don't worry. It's a thing about which nobody ever ought to give anybody any advice—so I'll give you some. Marry whoever you damn please. It'll be all the same after that oak I planted this morning is half grown."

" Gordon," he said, surprised, " I didn't suppose *you* were liberal."

" Liberal! Why, man alive! Do you think a fellow can live out of doors as I have lived, and see germs sprout, and see mountain ranges decay, and sit on a few glaciers, and swing a pick into a mother-lode—and *not* be liberal? Do you suppose ten-cent laws bother me when I'm up against the blind laws that made the law-makers?—laws that made life itself before Christ lived to conform to them? . . . I married where I loved. It chanced that my marriage with your sister didn't clash with the sanctified order of things in Manhattan town. But if your sister had been the maid who dresses her, and I had loved her, I'd have married her all the same and have gone about the pleasures and duties of procreation and conservation exactly as I go about 'em now. . . . I wonder how much the Almighty was thinking about Tenth Street when the first pair of anthropoids mated? *Nobilitas sola est atque unica*

virtus. If you love each other—*Noli pugnare duobus.*
. . . And I'm going into the woods to look for ginseng. Want to come?"

Neville went. Cameron and Stephanie, equipped
with buckskin gloves, a fox terrier, and digging apparatus, joined them just where the slender meadow brook
entered the woods.

"There are mosquitoes here!" exclaimed Cameron
wrathfully. "All day and every day I'm being
stung down town, and I'm not going to stand for it
here!"

Stephanie let him aid her to the top of a fallen log,
glancing back once or twice toward Neville, who was
sauntering forward among the trees, pretending to look
for ginseng.

"Do you notice how Louis has changed?" she said,
keeping her balance on the log. "I cannot bear to
see him so thin and colourless."

Cameron now entertained a lively suspicion how
matters stood, and knew that Stephanie also suspected;
but he only said, carelessly: "It's probably dissipation.
You know what a terrible pace he's been going from
the cradle onward."

She smiled quietly. "Yes, I know, Sandy. And I
know, too, that you are the only man who has been able
to keep up that devilish pace with him."

"I've led a horrible life," muttered Cameron darkly.

Stephanie laughed; he gave her his hand as she
stood balanced on the big log; she laid her fingers in
his confidently, looked into his honest face, still laughing, then sprang lightly to the ground.

"What a really good man you are!" she said tor-
mentingly.

" Oh, heaven ! If you call me that I'm really done for ! "

" Done for ? " she exclaimed in surprise. " How ? "

" Done for as far as you are concerned."

" I ? Why how, and with what am I concerned, Sandy ? I don't understand you."

But he only turned red and muttered to himself and strolled about with his hands in his pockets, kicking the dead leaves as though he expected to find something astonishing under them. And Stephanie glanced at him sideways once or twice, thoughtfully, curiously, but questioned him no further.

Gordon Collis pottered about in a neighbouring thicket; the fox terrier was chasing chipmunks. As for Neville he had already sauntered out of sight among the trees.

Stephanie, seated on a dry and mossy stump, pre-occupied with her own ruminations, looked up absently as Cameron came up to her bearing floral offerings.

" Thank you, Sandy," she said, as he handed her a cluster of wild blossoms. Then, fastening them to her waist, she glanced up mischievously:

" How funny you are ! You look and act like a little boy at a party presenting his first offering to the eternal feminine."

" It's my first offering," he said coolly.

" Oh, Sandy ! With *your* devilish record ! "

" Do you know," he said, " that I'm thirty-two years old ? And that you are twenty-two ? And that since you were twelve and I was twenty odd I've been in love with you ? "

She looked at him in blank dismay for a moment, then forced a laugh:

"Of course I know it, Sandy. It's the kind of love a girl cares most about——"

"It's really love," said Cameron, un-smiling—" the kind I'm afraid she doesn't care very much about."

"'If you'll place a lump of sugar on my nose, and say "when," I'll perform.'"

She hesitated, then met his gaze with a distressed smile:

"You don't really mean that, Sandy——"

"I've meant it for ten years. . . . But it doesn't matter——"

"Sandy! . . . It *does* matter—if——"

"No, it doesn't. . . . Come on and kick these leaves about and we'll make a million dollars in ginseng!"

But she remained seated, mute, her gaze a sorrowful interrogation which at length he could not pretend to ignore:

"Stephanie child, don't worry. I'm not worrying. I'm glad I told you. . . . Now just let me go on as I've always gone——"

"How *can* we?"

"Easily. Shut your eyes, breathe deeply, lifting both arms and lowering them while counting ten in German——"

"Sandy, don't be so foolish at—such a time."

"Such a time? What time is it?" pretending to consult his watch with great anxiety. Then a quick smile of relief spread over his features: "It's all right, Stephanie; it's my hour to be foolish. If you'll place a lump of sugar on my nose, and say ' when,' I'll perform."

There was no answering smile on her face.

"It's curious," she said, "how a girl can make a muddle of life without even trying."

"But just think what you might have done if you'd tried! You've much to be thankful for," he said gravely.

She raised her eyes, considering him:

"I wonder," she said, under her breath.

"Sure thing, Stephanie. You might have done worse; you might have married me. Throw away those flowers—there's a good girl—and forget what they meant."

Slowly, deliberately, blossom by blossom she drew them from her girdle and laid them on the moss beside her.

"There's one left," he said cheerfully. "Raus mit it!"

But she made no motion to detach it; appeared to be unconscious of it and of him as she turned her face and looked silently toward the place where Neville had disappeared.

An hour or two later, when Gordon was ready to return to the house, he shouted for Neville. Cameron also lifted up his voice in a series of prolonged howls.

But Neville was far beyond earshot, and still walking through woods and valleys and pleasant meadows in the general direction of the Estwich hills.

Somewhere there amid that soft rolling expanse of green was the woman who would never marry him. And it was now, at last, he decided that he would never take her on any other terms even though they were her own terms; that he must give her up to chance again as innocent as chance had given her into his brief keeping. No, she would never accept his terms and face the world with him as his wife. And so he must give her up. For he believed that, in him, the instinct of moral law had been too carefully developed ever to be deliberately ignored; he still believed marriage to be not only a rational social procedure, not only a human compromise and a divine convention, but the only possible sanctuary where love might dwell, and remain, and permanently endure inviolate.

CHAPTER XIV

THE Countess Hélène had taken her maid and gone
to New York on business for a day or two, leaving Valerie to amuse herself until her return.

Which was no hardship for Valerie. The only
difficulty lay in there being too much to do.

In the first place she had become excellent friends
with the farmer and had persuaded him to delegate to
her a number of his duties. She had to collect the
newly laid eggs, hunt up stolen nests, inspect and feed
the clucking, quacking, gobbling personnel of the barn-
yard which came crowding to her clear-voiced call.

As for the cattle, she was rather timid about venturing to milk since the Ogilvy's painful and undigni-
fied début as an amateur Strephon.

However, she assisted at pasture call accompanied
by a fat and lazy collie; and she petted and salted the
herd to her heart's content.

Then there were books and magazines to be read,
leisurely; and hammocks to lie in, while her eyes
watched the sky where clouds sailed in snowy squadrons
out of the breezy west.

And what happier company for her than her
thoughts—what tenderer companionship than her
memories; what more absorbing fellowship than the
little busy intimate reflections that came swarming
around her, more exciting, more impetuous, more ex-

quisitely disturbing as the hurrying, sunny hours sped away and the first day of June drew nigh?

She spent hours alone on the hill behind the house,

"And what happier company for her than her thoughts — what tenderer companionship than her memories?"

lying full length in the fragrant, wild grasses, looking across a green and sunlit world toward Ashuelyn.

She had told him not to attempt to come to Estwich; and, though she knew she had told him wisely, often and often there on her breezy hilltop she wished that she hadn't—wished that he would disregard her request—hoped he would—lay there, a dry grass stem between her lips, thinking how it would be if, suddenly, down there by—well, say down by that big oak, for example, a figure should stroll into view along the sheep-path. . . . And at first—just to prolong the tension—perhaps she wouldn't recognise him—just for a moment. Then, suddenly——

But she never got beyond that first blissful instant of recognition—the expression of his face—his quick spring forward—and she, amazed, rising to her feet and hastening forward to meet him. For she never pictured herself as standing still to await the man she loved.

When Hélène left, Valerie had the place to herself; and, without any disloyalty to the little countess, she experienced a new pleasure in the liberty of an indolence which exacted nothing of her.

She prowled around the library, luxuriously, dipping into inviting volumes; she strolled at hazard from veranda to garden, from garden to lawn, from lawn to farmyard.

About luncheon time she arrived at the house with her arms full of scented peonies, and spent a long while selecting the receptacles for them.

Luncheon was a deliciously lazy affair at which she felt at liberty to take her own time; and she did so, scanning the morning paper, which had just been delivered; making several bites of every cherry and strawberry, and being good to the three cats with asparagus ends and a saucer of chicken bouillon.

Later, reclining in the hammock, she mended a pair of brier-torn stockings; and when that thrifty and praiseworthy task was finished, she lay back and thought of Neville.

"She prowled around the library, luxuriously, dipping into inviting volumes."

But at what moment in any day was she ever entirely unconscious of him? Besides, she could always think of him better—summon him nearer—visualise him more clearly, when she was afield, the blue sky above her, the green earth under foot, and companioned only by memory.

So she went to her room, put on her stout little shoes and her walking skirt; braided her hair and made of it a soft, light, lustrous turban; and taking her dog-whip, ran down stairs.

The fat old collie came wagging up to the whistle, capered clumsily as in duty bound; but before she had entirely traversed the chestnut woods he basely deserted her and waddled back to the kitchen door where a thoughtful cook and a succulent bone were combinations not unknown.

Valerie missed him presently, and whistled; but the fat sybarite, if within earshot, paid no attention; and she was left to swing her dog-whip and stroll on alone.

Her direction lay along the most inviting by-roads and paths; and she let chance direct her feet through this friendly, sunny land where one little hill was as green as another, and one little brook as clear and musical as another, and the dainty, ferny patches of woodlands resembled one another.

It was a delight to scramble over stone walls; she adored lying flat and wriggling under murderous barbed-wire, feeling the weeds brush her face. When a brook was a little too wide to jump, it was ecstasy to attempt it. She got both shoes wet and loved it. Brambles plucked boldly at her skirt; wild forest blossoms timidly summoned her aside to kneel and touch them, but to let them live; squirrels threatened her and rushed madly up and down trees defying her; a redstart in vermilion and black, fussed about her where she sat,

416

"'Miss West!' he exclaimed. 'How on earth did you ever find your way into my woods?'"

closing and spreading its ornamental tail for somebody's benefit—perhaps for hers.

She was not tired; she did not suppose that she had wandered very far, but, glancing at her watch, she was surprised to find how late it was. And she decided to return.

After she had been deciding to return for about an hour it annoyed her to find that she could not get clear of the woods. It seemed preposterous; the woods could not be very extensive. As for being actually lost it seemed too absurd. Life is largely composed of absurdities.

There was one direction which she had not tried, and it lay along a bridle path, but whether north or south or east or west she was utterly unable to determine. She felt quite certain that Estwich could not lie either

417

way along that bridle-path which stretched almost a straight, dark way under the trees as far as she could see.

Vexed, yet amused, at her own stupid plight, she was standing in the road, trying to make up her mind to try it, when, far down the vista, a horseman appeared, coming on at a leisurely canter; and with a sigh of relief she saw her troubles already at an end.

He drew bridle abreast of her, stared, sprang from his saddle and, cap in hand, came up to her holding out his hand:

"Miss West!" he exclaimed. "How on earth did you ever find your way into my woods?"

"I don't know, Mr. Cardemon," she said, thankful to encounter even him in her dilemma. "I must have walked a great deal farther than I meant to."

"You've walked at least five miles if you came by road; and nobody knows how far if you came across country," he said, staring at her out of his slightly prominent eyes.

"I did come across country. And if you will be kind enough to start me toward home——"

"You mean to *walk* back!"

"Of course I do."

"I won't permit it!" he exclaimed. "It's only a little way across to the house and we'll just step over and I'll have a car brought around for you——"

"Thank you, I am not tired——"

"You are on my land, therefore you are my guest," he insisted. "I am not going to let you go back on foot——"

"Mr. Cardemon, if you please, I very much prefer to return in my own way."

"What an obstinate girl you are!" he said, with

his uncertain laugh, which never came until he had pre-judged its effect on the situation; but the puffy flesh above his white riding-stock behind his lobeless ears reddened, and a slow, thickish colour came into his face and remained under the thick skin.

"If you won't let me send you back in a car," he said, "you at least won't refuse a glass of sherry and a biscuit——"

"Thank you—I haven't time——"

"My housekeeper, Mrs. Munn, is on the premises," he persisted.

"You are very kind, but——"

"Oh, don't turn a man down so mercilessly, Miss West!"

"You are exceedingly amiable," she repeated, "but I must go at once."

He switched the weeds with his crop, then the un-certain laugh came:

"I'll show you a short cut," he said. His promi-nent eyes rested on her, passed over her from head to foot, then wandered askance over the young woodland.

"In which direction lies Estwich?" she asked, lift-ing her gaze to meet his eyes; but they avoided her as he answered, busy fumbling with a girth that required no adjustment:

"Over yonder,"—making a slight movement with his head. Then taking his horse by the head he said heartily:

"Awfully sorry you won't accept my hospitality; but if you won't you won't, and we'll try to find a short cut."

He led his horse out of the path straight ahead through the woods, and she walked beside him.

"Of course you know the way, Mr. Cardemon?"
she said pleasantly.

"I ought to—unless the undergrowth has changed
the looks of things since I've been through."

"How long is it since you've been through?"

"Oh, I can't just recollect," he said carelessly. "I
guess it will be all right."

For a while they walked steadily forward among
the trees; he talking to her with a frank and detached
amiability, asking about the people at Estwich, interested to hear that the small house-party had disin-
tegrated, surprised to learn that the countess had gone
to town.

"Are you entirely alone in the house?" he asked;
and his eyes seemed to protrude a little more than usual.

"Entirely," she said carelessly; "except for Binns
and his wife and the servants."

"Why didn't you 'phone a fellow to stop over to
lunch?" he asked, suddenly assuming a jovial manner
which their acquaintance did not warrant. "We country folk don't stand on ceremony you know."

"I did not know it," she said quietly.

His bold gaze rested on her again; again the uncertain laugh followed:

"If you'd ask me to dine with you to-night I'd take
it as a charming concession to our native informality.
What do you say, Miss West?"

She forced a smile, making a sign of negation with
her head, but he began to press her until his importunities and his short, abrupt laughter embarrassed
her.

"I couldn't ask anybody without permission from
my hostess," she said, striving to maintain the light,

careless tone which his changing manner toward her made more difficult for her.

"Oh, come, Miss West!" he said in a loud humorous voice; "don't pass me the prunes and prisms but be a good little sport and let a fellow come over to see you! You never did give me half a chance to know you, but you're hands across the table with that Ogilvy artist and José Querida——"

"I've known them rather longer than I have you, Mr. Cardemon."

"That's my handicap! I'm not squealing. All I want is to start in the race——"

"What race?" she asked coolly, turning on him a level gaze that, in spite of her, she could not maintain under the stare with which he returned it. And again the slight uneasiness crept over her and involuntarily she looked around her at the woods.

"How far is it now?" she inquired.

"Are you tired?"

"No. But I'm anxious to get back. Could you tell me how near to some road we are?"

He halted and looked around; she watched him anxiously as he tossed his bridle over his horse's neck and walked forward into a little glade where the late rays of the sun struck ruddy and warm on the dry grass.

"That's singular," he said as she went forward into the open where he stood; "I don't seem to remember this place."

"But you know about where we are, don't you?" she asked, resolutely suppressing the growing uneasiness and anxiety.

"Well—I am not perfectly certain." He kept his eyes off her while he spoke; but when she also turned and gazed helplessly at the woods encircling her, his glance stole toward her.

"You're not scared, are you?" he asked, and then laughed abruptly.

"Not in the slightest."

"Sure! You're a perfectly good sport. . . . I'll tell you—I'll leave my horse for one of my men to hunt up later, and we'll start off together on a good old-fashioned hike! Are you game?"

"Yes—if I only knew—if you were perfectly sure how to get to the edge of the woods. I don't see how you *can* be lost in your own woods——"

"I don't believe I am!" he said, laughing violently. "The Estwich road *must* be over in that direction. Come ahead, Miss West; the birds can cover us up if worst comes to worst!"

She went with him, entering the thicker growth with a quick, vigorous little stride as though energy and rapidity of motion could subdue the misgiving that threatened to frighten her sooner or later.

Over logs, boulders, gulleys, she swung forward, he supporting her from time to time in spite of her hasty assurance that she did not require aid.

Once, before she could prevent it, he grasped her and fairly swung her across a gulley; and again, as she gathered herself to jump, his powerful arm slipped around her body and he lowered her to the moss below, leaving her with red cheeks and a rapid heart to climb the laurel-choked ravine beside him.

It was breathless work; again and again, before she could prevent it, he forced his assistance on her; and in the abrupt, almost rough contact there was something that began at last to terrify her—weaken her—so that, at the top of the slope, she caught breathless at a tree and leaned against the trunk for a moment, closing her eyes.

"You poor little girl," he breathed close to her ear; and as her startled eyes flew open, he drew her into his arms.

For a second his congested face and prominent, pale eyes swam before her; then with a convulsive gasp she wrenched herself partly free and strained away from his grasp, panting.

"Let me go, Mr. Cardemon!"

"Look here, Valerie, you know I'm crazy about you——"

"Will you let me go?"

"Oh, come, little girl, I know who you are, all right! Be a good little sport and——"

"Let me go," she whispered between her teeth. Then his red, perspiring features—the prominent eyes and loose mouth drew nearer—nearer—and she struck blindly at the face with her dog-whip—twice with the lash and once with the stag-horn handle. And the next instant she was running.

He caught her at the foot of the slope; she saw blood on his cheek and puffy welts striping his distorted features, strove to strike him again, but felt her arm powerless in his grasp.

"Are you mad!" she gasped.

"Mad about *you!* For God's sake listen to me, Valerie! Batter me, tear me to pieces—and I won't care, if you'll listen to me a moment——"

She struggled silently, fiercely, to use her whip, to wrench herself free.

"I tell you I love you!" he said; "I'd go through

hell for you. You've got to listen — you've got to *know*——"

"You coward!" she sobbed.

"I don't care what you say to me if you'll listen a moment——"

"As Rita Tevis listened to you!" she said, white to the lips—"you murderer of souls!" And, as his grasp relaxed for a second, she tore her arm free, sprang forward and slashed him across the mouth with the lash.

Behind her she heard his sharp cry of pain, heard him staggering about in the underbrush. Terror winged her feet and she fairly flew along the open ridge and down through the dead leaves across a soft, green, marshy hollow, hearing him somewhere in the woods behind her, coming on at a heavy run.

For a long time she ran; and suddenly collapsed, falling in a huddled desperate heap, her slender hands catching at her throat.

At the foot of the hill she saw him striding hither and thither, examining the soft forest soil or halting to listen—then as though scourged into action, running aimlessly toward where she lay, casting about on every side like a burly dog at fault.

Once, when he stood not very far away, and she had hidden her face in her arms, trembling like a doomed thing—she heard him call to her—heard the cry burst from him as though in agony:

"Valerie, don't be afraid! I was crazy to touch you;—I'll let you cut me to pieces if you'll only answer me."

And again he shouted, in a voice made thin by fright: "For God's sake, Valerie, think of *me* for a moment. Don't run off like that and let people know what's happened to you!"

Then, in a moment, his heavy, hurried tread resounded; and he must have run very near to where she crouched, because she could hear him whimpering in his fear; but he ran on past where she lay, calling to her at intervals, until his frightened voice sounded at a distance and she could scarcely hear the rustle of the dead leaves under his hurrying tread.

Even then terror held her chained, breathing fast like a wounded thing, eyes bright with the insanity of her fear. She lay flat in the leaves, not stirring.

The last red sunbeams slanted through the woods, painting tree trunks crimson and running in fiery furrows through the dead leaves; the sky faded to rose-colour, to mauve; faintly a star shone.

For a long time now nothing had stirred in the woodland silence. And, as the star glimmered brighter through the branches, she shivered, moved, lay listening, then crawled a little way. Every sound that she made was a terror to her, every heart beat seemed to burst the silence.

It was dusk when she crept out at last into a stony road, dragging her limbs; a fine mist had settled over the fields; the air grew keener. Somewhere in the darkness cow-bells tinkled; overhead, through the damp sheet of fog, the veiled stars were still shining.

Her senses were not perfectly clear; she remembered falling once or twice—remembered seeing the granite posts and iron gates of a drive, and that lighted windows were shining dimly somewhere beyond. And she crept toward them, still stupid with exhaustion and fright. Then she was aware of people, dim shapes in the darkness—of a dog barking—of voices, a quick movement in the dusk—of a woman's startled exclamation.

Suddenly she heard Neville's voice—and a door opened, flooding her with yellow light where she stood swaying, dazed, deathly pale.

" Louis! " she said.

He sprang to her, caught her in his arms:

" Good God! What is the matter? "

She rested against him, her eyes listlessly watching the people swiftly gathering in the dazzling light.

" Where in the world—how did you get here!— where have you been—" His stammered words made him incoherent as he caught sight of the mud and dust on her torn waist and skirt.

Her eyes had closed a moment; they opened now with an effort. Once more she looked blindly at the people clustering around her—recognised his sister and Stephanie—divined that it was his mother who stood gazing at her in pallid consternation—summoned every atom of her courage to spare him the insult which a man's world had offered to her—found strength to ignore it so that no shadow of the outrage should fall through her upon him or upon those nearest to him.

" I lost my way," she said. Her white lips tried to smile; she strove to stand upright, alone; caught mechanically at his arm, the fixed smile still stamped on her lips. " I am sorry to—disturb anybody. . . . I was lost—and it grew dark. . . . I don't know my way —very well——"

She turned, conscious of some one's arm supporting her; and Stephanie said, in a low, pitiful voice:

"Lean back on me. You must let me help you to the house."

"Thank you—I won't go in. . . . If I could rest

"'Dearest,' he whispered, putting his arm around her, 'you must come with us.'"

—a moment—perhaps somebody—Mr. Neville—would help me to get home again——"

"Come with me, Miss West," whispered Stephanie, "I *want* you. Will you come to my room with me for a little while?"

She looked into Stephanie's eyes, turned and looked at Neville.

"Dearest," he whispered, putting his arm around her, "you must come with us."

She nodded and moved forward, steadily, between them both, and entered the house, head carried high on the slender neck, but her face was colourless under the dark masses of her loosened hair, and she swayed at the foot of the stairs, reaching out blindly at nothing—falling forward.

It was a dead weight that Neville bore into Stephanie's room. When his mother turned him out and closed the door behind him he stood stupidly about until his sister, who had gone into the room, opened the door and bade him telephone for Dr. Ogilvy.

"What has happened to her?" he asked, as though dazed.

"I don't know. I think you'd better tell Quinn to bring around the car and go for Dr. Ogilvy yourself."

It was a swift rush to Dartford through the night; bareheaded he bent forward beside the chauffeur, teeth set, every nerve tense and straining as though his very will power was driving the machine forward. Then there came a maddening slowing down through Dartford streets, a nerve-racking delay until Sam Ogilvy's giant brother had stowed away himself and his satchel in the tonneau; then slow speed to the town limits; a swift hurling forward into space that whirled blackly around them as the great acetylenes split the darkness and chaos roared in their ears.

Under the lighted windows the big doctor scrambled out and stamped upstairs; and Neville waited on the landing.

428

His father appeared below, looking up at him, and started to say something; but apparently changed his mind and went back into the living room, rattling his evening paper and coughing.

Cameron passed through the hallway, looked at him, but let him alone.

After a while the door opened and Lily came out.

" I'm not needed," she said; " your mother and Stephanie have taken charge."

" Is she going to be very ill? "

" Billy Ogilvy hasn't said anything yet."

" Is she conscious? "

" Yes, she is now."

" Has she said anything more? "

" No."

Lily stood silent a moment, gazing absently down at the lighted hall below, then she looked at her brother as though she, too, were about to speak, but, like her father, she reconsidered the impulse, and went away toward the nursery.

Later his mother opened the door very softly, let herself and Stephanie out, and stood looking at him, one finger across her lips, while Stephanie hurried away downstairs.

" She's asleep, Louis. Don't raise your voice——" as he stepped quickly toward her.

" Is it anything serious? " he asked in a low voice.

" I don't know what Dr. Ogilvy thinks. He is coming out in a moment. . . . " She placed one hand on her son's shoulder, reddening a trifle. " I've told William Ogilvy that she is a friend of——the family. He may have heard Sam talking about her when he was here last. So I thought it safer."

Neville brought a chair for his mother, but she shook her head, cautioning silence, and went noiselessly downstairs.

"'Well, Louis, what do you know about this?'"

Half an hour later Dr. Ogilvy emerged, saw Neville—walked up and inspected him, curiously.

"Well, Louis, what do you know about this?" he asked, buttoning his big thick rain-coat to the throat.

"Absolutely nothing, Billy, except that Miss

West, who is a guest of the Countess d'Enver at Estwich, lost her way in the woods.   How is she now?"

"All right," said the doctor, dryly.

"Is she conscious?"

"Perfectly."

"Awake?"

"Yes.   She won't be—long."

"Did she talk to you?"

"A little."

"What *is* the matter?"

"Fright.   And I'm wondering whether merely being lost in the woods is enough to have terrified a girl
like that?   Because, apparently, she is as superb a
specimen of healthy womanhood as this world manufac-
tures once in a hundred years.   How well do you know
her?"

"We are very close friends."

"H'm.   Did you suppose she was the kind of
woman to be frightened at merely being lost in a civil-
ised country?"

"No.   She has more courage—of all kinds—than
most women."

"Because," said the big doctor thoughtfully,
"while she was unconscious it took me ten minutes to
pry open her fingers and disengage a rather heavy dog-
whip from her clutch. . . . And there was some evi-
dences of blood on the lash and on the bone handle."

"What!" exclaimed Neville, amazed.

The doctor shrugged: "I don't know of any fierce
and vicious dogs between here and Estwich, either," he
mused.

"No, Cardemon keeps none.   And its mostly his
estate."

"Oh . . . Any—h'm!—vicious *men*—in his employment?"

"My God!" whispered Neville, "what do you
mean, Billy?"

"Finger imprints—black and blue—on both arms.
Didn't Miss West say anything that might enlighten
you?"

"No . . . She only said she had been lost. . . .
Wait a moment; I'm trying to think of the men Cardemon employs——"

He was ashy white and trembling, and the doctor
laid a steadying hand on his arm.

"Hold on, Louis," he said sharply, "it was no
worse than a fright. *Do you understand?* . . . And
do you understand, too, that an innocent and sensitive and modest girl would rather die than have
such a thing made public through your well-meant
activity? So there's nothing for anybody to do—
yet."

Neville could scarcely speak.

"Do you mean—she was attacked by some—man!"

"It looks like it. And—you'd better keep it from
your family—because she did. She's game to the core
—that little girl."

"But she—she'll tell me!" stammered Neville—
"she's *got* to tell me——"

"She won't if she can help it. Would it aid her
any if you found out who it was and killed him?—ran
for a gun and did a little murdering some pleasant
morning—just to show your chivalrous consideration
and devotion to her?"

"Are you asking me to let a beast like that go un-
punished?" demanded Neville violently.

"Oh, use your brains, Louis. He frightened her and she slashed him well for it. And, womanlike—after there was no more danger and no more necessity for pluck—she got scared and ran; and the farther she ran the more scared she became. Look here, Louis; look at me—squarely." He laid both ponderous hands on Neville's shoulders:

"Sam has told me all about you and Miss West—and I can guess how your family takes it. Can't you see why she had the pluck to remain silent about this thing? It was because she saw in it the brutal contempt of the world toward a woman who stood in that world alone, unsupported, unprotected. And she would not have you and your family know how lightly the world held the woman whom you love and wish to marry—not for her own sake alone—but for the sake of your family's pride—and yours."

His hands dropped from Neville's shoulders; he stood considering him for a moment in silence.

"I've told *you* because, if you are the man I think you are, you ought to know the facts. Forcing her to the humiliation of telling you will not help matters; filling this pup full of lead means an agony of endless publicity and shame for her, for your family, and for you. . . . He'll never dare remain in the same county with her after this. He's probably skedaddled by this time anyway." . . . Dr. Ogilvy looked narrowly at Neville. "Are you pretty sane, now?"

"Yes."

"You realise that gun-play is no good in this matter?"

"Y-yes."

"And you really are going to consider Miss West

before your own natural but very primitive desire to do murder? ''

Neville nodded.

" Knowing," added the doctor, " that the unspeakable cur who affronted her has probably taken to his heels? "

Neville, pale and silent, raised his eyes:

" Do you suspect anybody? "

" I don't know," said the doctor carelessly ;—" I'll just step over to the telephone and make an inquiry of Penrhyn Cardemon——"

He walked to the end of the big hall, unhooked the receiver, asked for Cardemon's house, got it.

Neville heard him say:

" This is Dr. Ogilvy. Is that you, Gelett? Isn't your master at home? "

· · · · · · ·

" What? Had to catch a train? "

· · · · · · ·

" Oh! A sudden matter of business."

· · · · · · ·

" I see. He's had a cable calling him to London. How long will he be away, Gelett? "

· · · · · · ·

" Oh, I see. You don't know. Very well. I only called up because I understood he required medical attention."

· · · · · · ·

" Yes—I understood he'd been hurt about the head and face, but I didn't know he had received such a— battering."

· · · · · · ·

" You say that his horse threw him in the big beech-woods? Was he really very much cut up? "

. . . .

" Pretty roughly handled, eh! All right. When you communicate with him tell him that Dr. Ogilvy and Mr. Neville, Jr., were greatly interested to know how badly he was injured. Do you understand? Well, don't forget. And you may tell him, Gelett, that as long as the scars remain, he'd better remain, too. Get it straight, Gelett; tell him it's my medical advice to remain away as long as he can—and a little longer. This climate is no good for him. Good-bye."

He turned from the telephone and sauntered toward Neville, who regarded him with a fixed stare.

" You see," he remarked with a shrug; and drew from his pocket a slightly twisted scarf pin—a big horse-shoe set with sapphires and diamonds—the kind of pin some kinds of men use in their riding-stocks.

" I've often seen him wearing it," he said carelessly. " Curious how it could have become twisted and entangled in Miss West's lace waist."

He held out the pin, turning it over reflectively as the facets of the gems caught and flashed back the light from the hall brackets.

" I'll drop it into the poor-box I think," he mused. " Cardemon will remain away so long that this pin will be entirely out of fashion when he returns."

After a few moments Neville drew a long, deep breath, and his clenched hands relaxed.

" Sure," commented the burly doctor. " That's right—feeling better—rush of common sense to the head. Well, I've got to go."

" Will you be here in the morning? "

"I think not. She'll be all right. If she isn't, send over for me."

"You don't think that the shock—the exhaustion——"

"Naw," said the big doctor with good-natured contempt; "she's going to be all right in the morning. . . . She's a lovely creature, isn't she? Sam said so. Sam has an eye for beauty. But, by jinks! I was scarcely prepared for such physical perfection—h'm! —or such fine and nice discrimination—or for such pluck. . . . God knows what people's families want these days. If the world mated properly our best families would be extinct in another generation. . . . You're one of 'em; you'd better get diligent before the world wakes up with a rush of common sense to its doddering old head." He gave him both hands, warmly, cordially: "Good-bye, Louis."

Neville said: "I want you to know that I'd marry her to-morrow if she'd have me, Billy."

The doctor lifted his eyebrows.

"Won't she?"

"No."

"Then probably you're not up to sample. A girl like that is no fool. She'll require a lot in a man. However, you're young; and you may make good yet."

"You don't understand, Billy——"

"Yes, I do. She wears a dinky miniature of you against her naked heart. Yes, I guess I understand. . . . And I guess she's that kind of a girl—all unselfishness and innocence, and generous perversity and —quixotic love. . . . It's too bad, Louis. I guess you're up against it for fair."

He surveyed the younger man, shook his head:

" They can't stand for her, can they? "

" No."

" And she won't stand for snaking you out of the fold. That's it, I fancy? "

" Yes."

" Too bad—too bad. She's a fine woman—a very fine little woman. That's the kind a man ought to ' marry and bother the Almighty with gratitude all the rest of his life. Well—well! Your family is your own after all; and I live in Dartford, thank God!—not on lower Fifth Avenue or Tenth Street."

He started away, halted, came back:

" Couldn't you run away with her? " he asked anxiously.

" She won't," replied Neville, unsmiling.

" I mean, violently. But she's too heavy to carry, I fancy—and I'll bet she's got the vigour of little old Diana herself. No—you couldn't do the Sabine act with her—only a club and the cave-man's gentle persuasion would help either of you. . . . Well—well, if they see her at breakfast it may help some. You know a woman makes or breaks herself at breakfast. That's why the majority of woman take it abed. I'm serious, Louis; no man can stand 'em—the majority."

Once more he started away, hesitated, came back.

" Who's this Countess that Sam is so crazy about? "

" A sweet little woman, well-bred, and very genuine and sincere."

" Never heard of her in Dartford," muttered the doctor.

Neville laughed grimly:

" Billy, Tenth Street and lower Fifth Avenue and Greenwich Village and Chelsea and Stuyvesant Square

—and Syringa Avenue, Dartford, are all about alike. Bird Centre is just as stupid as Manhattan; and there never was and never will be a republic and a democracy in any country on the face of this snob-cursed globe."

The doctor, very red, stared at him.

"By jinks!" he said, "I guess I'm one after all. Now, who in hell would suspect that!—after all the advice I've given you!"

"It was another fellow's family, that's all," said Neville wearily. "Theories work or they don't; only few care to try them on themselves or their own families—particularly when they devoutly believe in them."

"Gad! That's a stinger! You've got me going all right," said the doctor, wincing, "and you're perfectly correct. Here I've been practically counselling you to marry where your inclination led you, and let the rest go to blazes; and when it's a question of Sam doing something similar, I retire hastily across the river and establish a residence in Missouri. What a rotten, custom-ridden bunch of snippy-snappy-snobbery we are after all! . . . All the same—who *is* the Countess?"

Neville didn't know much about her.

"Sam's such an ass," said his brother, "and it isn't all snobbery on my part."

"The safest thing to do," said Neville bitterly, "is to let a man in love alone."

"Right. Foolish — damned foolish — but right! There is no greater ass than a wise one. Those who don't know anything at all are the better asses—and the happier."

And he went away down the stairs, muttering and gesticulating.

Mrs. Neville came to the door as he opened it to go

out. They talked in low voices for a few moments, then the doctor went out and Mrs. Neville called to Stephanie.

The girl came from the lighted drawing-room, and, together, the two women ascended the stairs.

Stephanie smiled and nodded to Neville, then continued on along the hall; but his mother stopped to speak to him.

" Go and sit with your father a little while," she said. " And don't be impatient with him, dear. He is an old man—a product of a different age and a simpler civilisation—perhaps a narrower one. Be patient and gentle with him. He really is fond of you and proud of you."

" Very well, mother. . . . Is anybody going to sit up with Valerie? "

" Stephanie insists on sleeping on the couch at the foot of her bed. I offered to sit up but she wouldn't let me. . . . You'll see that I'm called if anything happens, won't you? "

" Yes. Good-night, mother."

He kissed her, stood a moment looking at the closed door behind which lay Valerie—tried to realise that she did lie there under the same roof-tree that sheltered father, mother, and sister—then, with a strange thrill in his heart, he went downstairs.

Cameron passed him, on his upward way to slumberland.

" How's Miss West? " he asked cheerfully.

" Asleep, I think. Billy Ogilvy expects her to be all right in the morning."

" Good work! Glad of it. Tell your governor; he's been inquiring."

"Has he?" said Neville, with another thrill, and went into the living room where his father sat alone before the whitening ashes of the fire.

"Well, father!" he said, smiling.

The older man turned his head, then turned it away as his son drew up a chair and laid a stick across the andirons.

"It's turned a little chilly," he said.

"I have known of many a frost in May," said his father.

There was a silence; then his father slowly turned and gazed at him.

"How is—Miss West?" he asked stiffly.

"Billy Ogilvy says she will be all right to-morrow, father."

"Was she injured by her unfortunate experience?"

"A little briar-torn, I'm afraid. Those big beech woods are rather a puzzle to anybody who is not familiar with the country. No wonder she became frightened when it grew dark."

"It was—very distressing," nodded his father.

They remained silent again until Mr. Neville rose, took off his spectacles, laid aside *The Evening Post*, and held out his hand.

"Good-night, my son."

"Good-night, father."

"Yes—yes—good-night—good-night—to many, many. things, my son; old-fashioned things of no value any more—of no use to me, or you, or anybody any more."

He retained his son's hand in his, peering at him, dim-eyed, without his spectacles:

"The old order passes—the old ideas, the old beliefs—and the old people who cherished them—who know no others, needed no others. . . . Good-night, my son."

But he made no movement to leave, and still held to his son's hand:

"I've tried to live as blamelessly as my father lived, Louis—and as God has given me to see my way through life. . . . But—the times change so—change so. The times are perplexing; life grows noisier, and stranger and more complex and more violent every day around us—and the old require repose, Louis. Try to understand that."

"Yes, father."

The other looked at him, wearily:

"Your mother seems to think that your happiness in life depends on—what we say to you—this evening. Stephanie seems to believe it, too. . . . Lily says very little. . . . And so do I, Louis—very little . . . only enough to—to wish you—happiness. And so—good-night."

15

CHAPTER XV

It was barely daylight when Valerie awoke. She lay perfectly still, listening, remembering, her eyes wandering over the dim, unfamiliar room. Through thin silk curtains a little of the early light penetrated; she heard the ceaseless chorus of the birds, cocks crowing near and far away, the whimpering flight of pigeons around the eaves above her windows, and their low, incessant cooing.

Suddenly, through the foot-bars of her bed she caught sight of Stephanie lying sound asleep on the couch, and she sat up—swiftly, noiselessly, staring at her out of wide eyes from which the last trace of dreams had fled.

For a long while she remained upright among her pillows, looking at Stephanie, remembering, considering; then, with decision, she slipped silently out of bed, and went about her dressing without a sound.

In the connecting bath-room and dressing-room beyond she found her clothing gathered in a heap, evidently to be taken away and freshened early in the morning. She dared not brush it for fear of awakening Stephanie; her toilet was swift and simple; she clothed herself rapidly and stepped out into the hall, her rubber-soled walking shoes making no noise.

Below, the side-lights of the door made unbolting and unchaining easy; it would be hours yet before even

442

the servants were stirring, but she moved with infinite caution, stepping out onto the veranda and closing the door behind her without making the slightest noise.

Dew splashed her shoes as she hastened across the lawn. She knew the Estwich road even if there had been no finger-posts to point out her way.

The sun had not yet risen; woods were foggy; the cattle in the fields stood to their shadowy flanks in the thin mist; and everywhere, like the cheery rush of a stream, sounded the torrent of bird-music from bramble patch and alder-swale, from hedge and orchard and young woodland.

It was not until she had arrived in sight of Estwich Corners that she met the first farmer afield; and, as she turned into the drive, the edge of the sun sent a blinding search-light over a dew-soaked world, and her long shadow sprang into view, streaming away behind her across the lawn.

To her surprise the front door was open and a harnessed buck-board stood at the gate; and suddenly she recollected with a hot blush that the household must have been amazed and probably alarmed by her non-appearance the night before.

Hélène's farmer and her maid came out as she entered the front walk, and, seeing her, stood round-eyed and gaping.

"I got lost and remained over night at Mrs. Collis's," she said, smiling. "Now, I'd like a bath if you please and some fresh clothing for travelling, because I am obliged to go to the city, and I wish to catch the earliest train.

When at last it was plain to them that she was alive and well, Hélène's maid, still trembling, hastened to draw a bath for her and pack the small steamer trunk; and the farmer sat down on the porch and waited, still more or less shaken by the anxiety which had sent him pottering about the neighbouring woods and fields with a lantern the night before, and had aroused him to renewed endeavour before sunrise.

Bathed and freshly clothed, Valerie hastened into the pretty library, seated herself at the desk, pushed up her veil, and wrote rapidly:

"MY DEAR MRS. COLLIS: My gratitude to you, to Mrs. Neville, and to Miss Swift is none the less real because I am acknowledging it by letter. Besides, I am very certain that you would prefer it so.

"You and your family have been kindness itself to me in my awkward and painful dilemma; you have sheltered me and provided medical attendance; and I am deeply in your debt.

"Had matters been different I need scarcely say that it would have been a pleasure for me to personally acknowledge to you and your family my grateful appreciation.

"But I am very sure that I could show my gratitude in no more welcome manner than by doing what I have done this morning and by expressing that obligation to you in writing.

"Before I close may I ask you to believe that I had no intention of seeking shelter at your house? Until I heard Mr. Neville's voice I had no idea where I was. I merely made my way toward the first lighted windows that I saw, never dreaming that I had come to Ashuelyn.

"I am sorry that my stupid misadventure has

444

caused you and your family so much trouble and annoyance. I feel it very keenly—more keenly because of your kindness in making the best of what must have been to you and your family a most disagreeable episode.

"May I venture to express to you my thanks to Miss Swift who so generously remained in my room last night? I am deeply sensible of her sweetness to an unwelcome stranger—and of Mrs. Neville's gentle manner toward one who, I am afraid, has caused her much anxiety.

"To the very amiable physician who did so much to calm a foolish and inexcusable nervousness, I am genuinely grateful. If I knew his name and address I would write and properly acknowledge my debt.

"There is one thing more before I close: I am sorry that I wrote you so ungraciously after receiving your last letter. It would have been perfectly easy to have thanked you courteously, whatever private opinion I may have entertained concerning a matter about which there may be more than my own opinion.

"And now, please believe that I will never again voluntarily cause you and your family the slightest uneasiness or inconvenience; and believe me, too, if you care to,   Very gratefully yours,
                        "VALERIE WEST."

She directed and sealed the letter, then drew toward her another sheet of paper:

"DEAREST: I could die of shame for having blundered into your family circle. I dare not even consider what they must think of me now. *You* will know how innocently and unsuspiciously it was done—how utterly impossible it would have been for me to have voluntarily committed such an act even in the last extremity. But what *they* will think of my appearance at your door last night, I don't know and I dare not surmise. I have done all I could; I have rid them of me, and I have written to your sister to thank her and your family for their very real kindness to the last woman in the world whom they would have willingly chosen to receive and entertain.

"Dear, I didn't know I had nerves; but this experience seems to have developed them. I am perfectly well, but the country here has become distasteful to me, and I am going to town in a few minutes. I want to get away—I want to go back to my work—earn my living again—live in blessed self-respect where, as a worker, I have the right to live.

"Dearest, I am sorry about not meeting you at the station and going back to town with you. But I simply cannot endure staying here after last night. I suppose it is weak and silly of me, but I feel now as though your family would never be perfectly tranquil again until I am out of their immediate vicinity. I cannot convey to you or to them how sorry and how distressed I am that this thing has occurred.

"But I can, perhaps, make you understand that I love you, dearly—love you enough to give myself to you—love you enough to give you up forever.

"And it is to consider what is best, what to do, that I am going away quietly somewhere by myself to think it all out once more—and to come to a final decision before the first of June.

"I want to search my heart, and let God search it for any secret selfishness and unworthiness that might sway me in my choice—any overmastering love for you that might blind me. When I know myself, you shall know me. Until then I shall not write you; but sometime before the first of June—or on that day, you shall know and I shall know how I have decided wherein I may best serve you—whether by giving or withholding —whether by accepting or refusing forever all that I care for in the world—you, Louis, and the love you have given me.

"VALERIE WEST."

She sealed and directed this, laid it beside the other, and summoned the maid:

"Have these sent at once to Ashuelyn," she said; "let Jimmy go on his bicycle. Are my things ready? Is the buck-board still there? Then I will leave a note for the Countess."

And she scribbled hastily:

"HÉLÈNE DEAR: I've got to go to town in a hurry on matters of importance, and so I am taking a very unceremonious leave of you and of your delightful house.

"They'll tell you I got lost in the woods last night, and I did. It was too stupid of me; but no harm came of it—only a little embarrassment in accepting a night's shelter at Ashuelyn among people who were everything that was hospitable, but who must have been anything but delighted to entertain me.

"In a few weeks I shall write you again. I have not exactly decided what to do this summer. I may go abroad for a vacation as I have saved enough to do so in an economical manner; and I should love to see the

French cathedrals. Perhaps, if I so decide, you might be persuaded to go with me.

"However, it is too early to plan yet. A matter of utmost importance is going to keep me busy and secluded for a week or so. After that I shall come to some definite decision; and then you shall hear from me.

"In the meanwhile—I have enjoyed Estwich and you immensely. It was kind and dear of you to ask me. I shall never forget my visit.

"Good-bye, Hélène dear.

"Valerie West."

This note she left on Hélène's dresser, then ran downstairs and sprang into the buck-board.

They had plenty of time to catch the train; and on the train she had plenty of leisure for reflection. But she could not seem to think; a confused sensation of excitement invaded her mind and she sat in her velvet armed chair alternately shivering with the memory of Cardemon's villainy, and quivering under the recollection of her night at Ashuelyn.

Rita was not at home when she came into their little apartment. The parrot greeted her, flapping his brilliant wings and shrieking from his perch; the goldfish goggled his eyes and swam 'round and 'round. She stood still in the centre of her room looking vacantly about her. An immense, overwhelming sense of loneliness came over her; she turned as the rush of tears blinded her and flung herself full length among the pillows of her bed.

Her first two or three days in town were busy ones; she had her accounts to balance, her inventories to take, her mending to do, her modest summer wardrobe to acquire, letters to write and to answer, engagements to make, to fulfill, to postpone; friends to call on and to

"The parrot greeted her, flapping his brilliant wings and shrieking from his perch."

receive, duties in regard to the New Idea Home to attend to.

Also, the morning after her arrival came a special delivery letter from Neville:

"It was a mistake to go, dear, because, although you could not have known it, matters have changed most happily for us. You were a welcome guest in my sister's house; you would have been asked to remain after your visit at Estwich was over. My family's sentiments are changing—have changed. It requires only you yourself to convince them. I wish you had remained, although your going so quietly commanded the respect of everybody. They all are very silent about it and about you, yet I can see that they have been affected most favourably by their brief glimpse of you.

"As for your wishing to remain undisturbed for a few days, I can see no reason for it now, dear, but of course I shall respect your wishes.

"Only send me a line to say that the month of June will mean our marriage. Say it, dear, because there is now no reason to refuse."

To which she answered:

"Dearest among all men, no family's sentiments change over night. Your people were nice to me and I have thanked them. But, dear, I am not likely to delude myself in regard to their real sentiments concerning me. Too deeply ingrained, too basic, too essentially part of themselves and of their lives are the creeds, codes, and beliefs which, in spite of themselves, must continue to govern their real attitude toward such a girl as I am.

"It is dear of you to wish for us what cannot be; it is kind of them to accept your wish with resignation.

"But I have told you many times, my darling, that I would not accept a status as your wife at any cost to you or to them—and I can read between the lines, even if I did not know, what it would cost them and you. And so, very gently, and with a heart full of gratitude and love for you, I must decline this public honour.

"But, God willing, I shall not decline a lifetime devoted to you when you are not with them. That is all I can hope for; and it is so much more than I ever dreamed of having, that, to have you at all—even for a part of the time—even for a part of my life, is enough. And I say it humbly, reverently, without ignoble envy or discontent for what might have been had you and I been born to the same life amid the same surroudings.

"Don't write to me again, dear, until I have determined what is best for us. Before the first day of summer, or on that day, you will know. And so will I.

"My life is such a little thing compared to yours— of such slight value and worth that sometimes I think I am considering matters too deeply—that if I simply fling it in the scales the balance will scarcely be altered —the splendid, even tenor of your career will scarcely swerve a shade.

"Yet my life is already something to you; and besides it is all I have to give you; and if I am to give it— if it is adding an iota to your happiness for me to give it—then I must truly treat it with respect, and deeply consider the gift, and the giving, and if it shall be better for you to possess it, or better that you never shall.

"And whatever I do with myself, my darling, be certain that it is of you I am thinking and not of the girl who loves you.

"V."

By degrees she cleared up her accounts and set her small house in order.

Rita seemed to divine that something radical was in progress of evolution, but Valerie offered no confidence, and the girl, already deeply worried over John Burleson's condition, had not spirit enough to meddle.

"Sam Ogilvy's brother is a wonder on tubercular cases," she said to Valerie, "and I'm doing my best to get John to go and see him at Dartford."

"Won't he?"

"He says he will, but you know how horridly untruthful men are. And now John is slopping about with his wet clay again as usual—an order for a tomb in Greenwood—poor boy, he had better think how best to keep away from tombs."

"Why, Rita!" said Valerie, shocked.

"I can't help it; I'm really frightened, dear. And you know well enough I'm no flighty alarmist. Besides, somehow, I feel certain that Sam's brother would tell John to go to Arizona "—she pointed piteously to her trunk: "It's packed; it has been packed for weeks. I'm all ready to go with him. Why can't a man mould clay and chip marble and cast bronze as well in Arizona as in this vile pest-hole?"

Valerie sat with folded hands looking at her.

"How do you think *you* could stand that desolation?"

"Arizona?"

"Yes."

"There is another desolation I dread more."

"Do you really love him so?"

Rita slowly turned from the window and looked at her.

"Yes," she said.

452

"'And they—the majority of them—are, after all, just men.'"

"Does he know it, Rita?"

"No, dear."

"Do you think—if he did——"

"No. . . . How could it be—after what has happened to me?"

"You would tell him?"

"Of course. I sometimes wonder whether he has not already heard—something—from that beast——"

"Does John know him?"

"He has done two fountains for his place at El Naúar. He had several other things in view—" she shrugged—"but *The Mohave* sailed suddenly with its owner for a voyage around the world—so John was told;—and—Valerie, it's the first clear breath of relief I've drawn since Penrhyn Cardemon entered John's studio."

"I didn't know he had ever been there."

"Yes; twice."

"Did you see him there?"

"Yes. I nearly dropped. At first he did not recognise me—I was very young—when——"

"Did he speak to you?"

"Yes. I managed to answer. John was not looking at me, fortunately. . . . After that he wrote to me —and I burned the letter. . . . It was horrible; he said that José Querida was his guest at El Naúar, and he asked me to get you because you knew Querida, and be his guest for a week end. . . . I cried that night; you heard me."

"Was *that* it!" asked Valerie, very pale.

"Yes; I was too wretched to tell you."

Valerie sat silent, her teeth fixed in her lower lip. Then:

455

resentment is really more of contempt than of anger—and perhaps more of pity than of either."

Rita said: "I cannot feel as charitably. . . . *You* still have that right."

"Rita! Rita!" she said softly, "we both have loved men, you with the ignorance and courage of a child—I with less ignorance and with my courage as yet untested. Where is the difference between us—if we love sincerely?"

Rita leaned forward and looked at her searchingly: "Do you mean to do—what you said you would?"

"Yes."

"Why?"

"Because he wants me."

Rita sprang to her feet and began pacing the floor.

"I will not have it so!" she said excitedly, "I will not have it so! If he is a man—a real man—he will not have it so, either. If he will, he does not love you; mark what I say, Valerie—he does not love you enough. No man can love a woman enough to accept that from her; it would be a paradox, I tell you!"

"He loves me enough," said Valerie, very pale. "He could not love me as I care for him; it is not in a man to do it, nor in any human being to love as I love him. You don't understand, Rita. I *must* be a part of him—not very much, because already there is so much to him—and I am so—so unimportant."

"You are more important than he is," said Rita fiercely—"with all your fineness and loyalty and divine sympathy and splendid humility—with your purity and your loveliness; and in spite of his very lofty intellect and his rather amazing genius, and his inherited social respectability—*you* are the more important to the happiness and welfare of this world—even to the humblest corner in it!"

"Rita! Rita! What wild, partisan nonsense you are talking!"

'His thoughts were mostly centred on Valerie."

"Oh, Valerie, Valerie, if you only knew! If you only knew!"

Querida called next day. Rita was at home but flatly refused to see him.

"Tell Mr. Querida," she said to the janitor, "that neither I nor Miss West are at home to him, and that if he is as nimble at riddles as he is at mischief he can guess this one before his friend Mr. Cardemon returns from a voyage around the world."

Which reply slightly disturbed Querida.

All during dinner—and he was dining alone—he considered it; and his thoughts were mostly centred on Valerie.

Somehow, some way or other he must come to an understanding with Valerie West. Somehow, some way, she must be brought to listen to him. Because, while he lived, married or single, poor or wealthy, he would never rest, never be satisfied, never wring from life the last drop that life must pay him, until this woman's love was his.

He loved her as such a man loves; he had no idea of letting that love for her interfere with other ambitions.

Long ago, when very poor and very talented and very confident that the world, which pretended to ignore him, really knew in its furtive heart that it owed him fame and fortune and social position, he had determined to begin the final campaign with a perfectly suitable marriage.

That was all years ago; and he had never swerved in his determination—not even when Valerie West surprised his life in all the freshness of her young beauty.

And, as he sat there leisurely over his claret, he reflected, easily, that the time had come for the marriage, and that the woman he had picked out was perfectly suitable, and that the suitable evening to inform her was the present evening.

Mrs. Hind-Willet was prepossessing enough to interest him, clever enough to stop gaps in a dinner table conversation, wealthy enough to permit him a liberty of rejecting commissions, which he had never before dared to exercise, and fashionable enough to carry for him what could not be carried through his own presentable good looks and manners and fame.

This last winter he had become a frequenter of her house on Sixty-third Street; and so carelessly assiduous, and so delightfully casual had become his attentions to that beautifully groomed widow, that his footing with her was already an intimacy, and his portrait of her, which he had given her, had been the sensation of the loan exhibition at the great Interborough Charity Bazaar.

He was neither apprehensive nor excited as he calmly finished his claret. He was to drop in there after dinner to discuss with her several candidates as architects for the New Idea Home.

So when he was entirely ready he took his hat and stick and departed in a taxicab, pleasantly suffused with a gentle glow of anticipation. He had waited many years for such an evening as this was to be. He was a patient and unmoral man. He could wait longer for Valerie,—and for the first secret blow at the happiness and threatened artistic success of Louis Neville.

So he rolled away in his taxi very comfortably, savouring his cigarette, indolently assured of his reception in a house which it would suit him perfectly to inhabit when he cared to.

Only one thing worried him a little—the short note he had received from his friend Penrhyn Cardemon, saying rather brusquely that he'd made up his mind not to have his portrait painted for five thousand dollars, and that he was going off on *The Mohave* to be gone a year at least.

Which pained Querida, because Cardemon had not only side-stepped what was almost a commission, but he had, also, apparently forgotten his invitation to spend the summer on *The Mohave*—with the understanding that Valerie West was also to be invited.

However, everything comes in its season; and this did not appear to be the season for ripe commissions and yachting enterprises; but it certainly seemed to be the season for a judicious matrimonial enterprise.

And when Mrs. Hind-Willet received him in a rose-tinted reception corner, audaciously intimate and secluded, he truly felt that he was really missing something of the pleasures of the chase, and that it was a little too easy to be acutely enjoyable.

However, when at last he had gently retained her hand and had whispered, " Alma," and had let his big, dark, velvet eyes rest with respectful passion upon her smaller and clearer and blacker ones, something somewhere in the machinery seemed to go wrong—annoyingly wrong.

Because Mrs. Hind-Willet began to laugh—and evidently was trying not to—trying to remain very serious; but her little black eyes were glistening with tears of suppressed mirth, and when, amazed and offended, he would have withdrawn his hand, she retained it almost convulsively:

" José! I *beg* your pardon!—I truly do. It is perfectly horrid and unspeakable of me to behave this way; but listen, child! I am forty; I am perfectly contented not to marry again; *and* I don't love you. So, my poor José, what on earth am I to do if I don't laugh a little. I *can't* weep over it you know."

The scarlet flush faded from his olive skin. "Alma," he began mournfully, but she only shook her head, vigorously.

"Nonsense," she said. "You like me for a sufficient variety of reasons. And to tell you the truth I suspect that I am quite as madly in love with you as you actually are with me. No, no, José. There are too many—discrepancies—of various kinds. I have too little to gain!—to be horribly frank—and you— alas!—are a very cautious, very clever, and admirably sophisticated young man. . . . There, there! I am not really accusing you—or blaming you—very much. . . . I'd have tried the same thing in your place—yes, indeed I would. . . . But, José dear, if you'll take the mature advice of fair, plump, and forty, you'll let the lesser ambition go.

"A clever wealthy woman nearer your age, and on the edge of things—with you for a husband, ought to carry you and herself far enough to suit you. And there'd be more amusement in it, believe me. . . . And now—you may kiss my hand—very good-humoredly and respectfully, and we'll talk about those architects. Shall we?"

For twenty-four hours Querida remained a profoundly astonished man. Examine, in retrospective, as he would, the details of the delicately adjusted machinery which for so many years had slowly but surely turned the interlocking cog-wheels of destiny for him, he could not find where the trouble had been—could discover no friction caused by neglect of lubricants; no over-oiling, either; no flaw.

Wherein lay the trouble? Based on what error was

his theory that the average man could marry anybody he chose? Just where had he miscalculated?

He admitted that times changed very fast; that the world was spinning at a rate that required nimble wits to keep account of its revolutions. But his own wits were nimble, almost feminine in the rapid delicacy of their intuition—*almost* feminine, but not quite. And he felt, vaguely, that there lay his mistake in engaging a woman with a woman's own weapons; and that the only chance a man has is to perplex her with his own.

The world was spinning rapidly; times changed very fast, but not as fast as women were changing in the Western World. For the self-sufficient woman—the self-confident, self-sustaining individual, not only content but actually preferring autonomy of mind and body, was a fact in which José Querida had never really ever believed. No sentimentalist does or really can. And all creators of things artistic are, basically, sentimentalists.

Querida's almond-shaped, velvet eyes had done their share for him in his time; they were merely part of a complex machinery which included many exquisitely adjusted parts which could produce at will such phenomena as temporary but genuine sympathy and emotion: a voice controlled and modulated to the finest nuances; a grace of body and mind that resembled inherent delicacy; a nervous receptiveness and intelligence almost supersensitive in its recognition of complicated ethical problems. It was a machinery which could make of him any manner of man which the opportunism of the particular moment required. Yet, with all this, in every nerve and bone and fibre he adored material and intellectual beauty, and physical suffering in others actually distressed him.

Now, reviewing matters, deeply interested to find the microscopic obstruction which had so abruptly stopped the machinery of destiny for him, he was modest enough and sufficiently liberal-minded to admit to himself that Alma Hind-Willet was the exception that proved this rule. There *were* women so constructed that they had become essentially unresponsive. Alma was one. But, he concluded that if he lived a thousand years he was not likely to encounter another.

And the following afternoon he called upon Mrs. Hind-Willet's understudy, the blue-eyed little Countess d'Enver.

Hélène d'Enver was superintending the definite closing of her beautiful duplex apartments—the most beautiful in the great château-like, limestone building. And José Querida knew perfectly well what the rents were.

"Such a funny time to come to see me," she had said laughingly over the telephone; "I'm in a dreadful state with skirts pinned up and a motor-bonnet over my hair, but I will *not* permit my maids to touch the porcelains; and if you really wish to see me, come ahead."

He really wished to. Besides he adored her Ming porcelains and her Celedon, and the idea of any maid touching them almost gave him heart-failure. He himself possessed one piece of Ming and a broken fragment of Celedon. Women had been married for less.

She was very charming in her pinned-up skirts and her dainty head-gear, and she welcomed him and intrusted him with specimens which sent pleasant shivers down his flexible spine.

And, together, they put away many scores of specimens which were actually priceless, inasmuch as any rumour of a public sale would have excited amateurs to the verge of lunacy, and almost any psychopathic might have established a new record for madness at an auction of this matchless collection.

They breathed easier when the thrilling task was ended; but emotion still enchained them as they seated themselves at a tea-table—an emotion so deep on Hélène's part that she suffered Querida to retain the tips of her fingers for an appreciable moment when transferring sugar to his cup. And she listened, with a smile almost tremulous, to the fascinating music of his voice, charmingly attuned and modulated to a pitch, which, somehow, seemed to harmonise with the very word, Celedon.

"I am so surprised," she said softly—but his dark eyes noted that she was still busy with her tea paraphernalia—"I scarcely know what to think, Mr. Querida——"

"Think that I love you——" breathed Querida, his dark and beautiful head very near to her blond one.

"I—am—thinking of it. . . . But——"

"Hélène," he whispered musically;—and suddenly stiffened in his chair as the maid came clattering in over the rugless and polished parquet to announce Mr. Ogilvy, followed *san façon* by that young man, swinging a straw hat and a malacca stick.

"Sam!" said the pretty Countess, changing countenance.

"Hello, Hélène! How-do, Querida! I heard you were temporarily in town, dear lady—" He kissed a hand that was as faltering and guilty as the irresolute eyes she lifted to his.

Ten minutes later Querida took his leave. He dismissed the expensive taxi which had been devouring time outside, and walked thoughtfully away down the fashionable street.

Because the machinery had chanced to clog twice did not disturb his theory; but the trouble with him was local; he was intensely and personally annoyed, nervous, irritated unspeakably. Because, except for Valerie, these two, Alma Hind-Willet and Hélène d'Enver, were the only two socially and financially suitable women in whom he took the slightest physical interest.

There is, in all women, one moment—sometimes repeated—in which a sudden yielding to caprice sometimes overturns the logical plans laid out and inexorably followed for half a lifetime. And there was much of the feminine about Querida.

And it chanced to happen on this day—when no doubt all unsuspected and unperceived some lurking jettatura had given him the evil eye—that he passed by hazard through the block where Valerie lived, and saw her mounting the steps.

"Why, José!" she exclaimed, a trifle confused in her smiling cordiality as he sprang up the steps behind her—for Rita's bitterness, if it had not aroused in her suspicions, had troubled her in spite of her declaration of unbelief.

He asked for a cup of tea, and she invited him. Rita was in the room when they entered; and she stood up coolly, coolly returned Querida's steady glance and salutation with a glance as calm, as detached, and as intelligent as a surgeon's.

Neither he nor she referred to his recent call; he was perfectly self-possessed, entirely amiable with that serene and level good-humour which sometimes masks a defiance almost contemptuous.

But Rita's engagements required her to leave very shortly after his advent; and before she went out she deliberately waited to catch Valerie's eye; and Valerie coloured deeply under her silent message.

Then Rita went away with a scarcely perceptible nod to Querida; and when, by the clock, she had been gone twenty minutes, Querida, without reason, without preparation, and perfectly aware of his moment's insanity, yielded to a second's flash of caprice—the second that comes once in the lives of all women—and now, in the ordered symmetry of his life, had come to him.

"Valerie," he said, "I love you. Will you marry me?"

She had been leaning sideways on the back of her chair, one hand supporting her cheek, gazing almost listlessly out of the open window.

She did not stir, nor did her face alter, but, very quietly she turned her head and looked at him.

He spoke, breathlessly, eloquently, persuasively, and well; the perfect machinery was imitating for him a single-minded, ardent, honourable young man, intelligent enough to know his own mind, manly enough to speak it. The facsimile was flawless.

He had finished and was waiting, long fingers gripping the arms of his chair; and her face had altered only to soften divinely, and her eyes were very sweet and untroubled.

"I am glad you have spoken this way to me, José. Something has been said about you—in connection with

467

Mr. Cardemon—which disturbed me and made me very sad and miserable, although I would not permit myself to believe it. . . . And now I know it was a mistake— because you have asked me to be your wife."

She sat looking at him, the sadness in her eyes emphasised by the troubled smile curving her lips:

"I couldn't marry you, José, because I am not in love with you. If I were I would do it. . . . But I do not care for you that way."

For an instant some inner flare of madness blinded his brain and vision. There was, in his face, something so terrible that Valerie unconsciously rose to her feet, bewildered, almost stunned.

"I want you," he said slowly.

"José! What in the world——"

His dry lips moved, but no articulate sound came from them. Suddenly he sprang to his feet, and out of his twisted, distorted mouth poured a torrent of passion, of reproach, of half-crazed pleading—incoherency tumbling over incoherency, deafening her, beating in upon her, till she swayed where she stood, holding her arms up as though to shield herself.

The next instant she was straining, twisting in his arms, striving to cry out, to wrench herself free to keep her feet amid the crash of the overturned table and a falling chair.

"José! Are you insane?" she panted, tearing herself free and springing toward the door. Suddenly she halted, uttered a cry as he jumped back to block her way. The low window-ledge caught him under both knees; he clutched at nothing, reeled backward and outward and fell into space.

For a second she covered her white face with both

hands, then turned, dragged herself to the open window, forced herself to look out.

He lay on his back on the grass in the rear yard, and the janitor was already bending over him. And when she reached the yard Querida had opened both eyes.

Later the ambulance came, and with its surgeon came a policeman. Querida, lying with his head on her lap, opened his eyes again:

" I was—seated—on the window-ledge," he said with difficulty—" and overbalanced myself. . . . Caught the table—but it fell over. . . . That's all."

The eyes in his ghastly face closed wearily, then fluttered:

" Awfully sorry, Valerie—make such a mess—in your house."

" Oh-h—José," she sobbed.

After that they took him away to the Presbyterian Hospital; and nobody seemed to find very much the matter with him except that he'd been badly shocked.

But the next day all sensation ceased in his body from the neck downward.

And they told Valerie why.

For ten days he lay there, perfectly conscious, patient, good-humored, and his almond-shaped and hollow eyes rested on Valerie and Rita with a fatalistic serenity subtly tinged with irony.

John Burleson came to see him, and cried. After he left, Querida said to Valerie:

" John and I are destined to remain near neighbours; his grief is well meant, but a trifle premature."

" You are not going to die, José! " she said gently.

But he only smiled.

Ogilvy came, Annan came, the Countess Hélène, and

469

even Mrs. Hind-Willet. He inspected them all with his shadowy and mysterious smile, answered them gently; deep in his sunken eyes a sombre amusement seemed to dwell. But there was in it no bitterness.

Then Neville came. Valerie and Rita were absent that day but their roses filled the private ward-room with a hint of the coming summer.

Querida lay looking at Neville, the half smile resting on his pallid face like a slight shadow that faintly waxed and waned with every breath he drew.

"Well," he said quietly, "you are the man I wished to see."

"Querida," he said, deeply affected, "this thing isn't going to be permanent——"

"No; not permanent. It won't last, Neville. Nothing does last. . . . unless you can tell me whether my pictures are going to endure. Are they? I know that you will be as honest with me as I was—dishonest with you. I will believe what you say. Is my work destined to be permanent?"

"Don't you know it is?"

"I thought so. . . . But *you* know. Because, Neville, you are the man who is coming into what was mine, and what will be your own;—and you are coming into more than that, Neville, more than I ever could have attained. Now answer me; will my work live?"

"Always," said Neville simply.

Querida smiled:

"The rest doesn't matter then. . . . Even Valerie doesn't matter. . . . But you may hand me one of her roses. . . . No, a bud, if you don't mind—unopened."

When it was time for Neville to go Querida's smile

had faded and the pink rose-bud lay wilted in his fingers.

"It is just as well, Neville," he said. "I couldn't have endured your advent. Somebody *has* to be first; I was—as long as I lived. . . . It is curious how acquiescent a man's mind becomes—when he's like this. I never believed it possible that a man really could die without regret, without some shadow of a desire to live. Yet it is that way, Neville. . . . But a man must lie dying before he can understand it."

A highly tinted uncle from Oporto arrived in New York just in time to see Querida alive. He brought with him a parrot.

"Send it to Mrs. Hind-Willet," whispered Querida with stiffening lips; "*uno lavanta la caça y otro la mata.*"

A few minutes later he died, and his highly coloured uncle from Oporto sent the bird to Mrs. Hind-Willet and made the thriftiest arrangement possible to transport what was mortal of a great artist to Oporto—where a certain kind of parrot comes from.

CHAPTER XVI

On the morning of the first day of June Neville came into his studio and found there a letter from Valerie:

"Dearest: I am not keeping my word to you; I am asking you for more time; and I know you will grant it.

"José Querida's death has had a curious effect on me. I was inclined to care very sincerely for him; I comprehended him better than many people, I think. Yet there was much in him that I never understood. And I doubt that he ever entirely understood himself.

"I believe that he was really a great painter, Louis —and have sometimes thought that his character was mediæval at the foundations—with five centuries of civilisation thinly deposited over the bed-rock. . . . In him there seemed to be something primitive; something untamable, and utterly irreconcilable with the fundamental characteristics of modern man.

"He was my friend. . . . Friendship, they say, is a record of misunderstandings; and it was so with us. But may I tell you something? José Querida loved me —in his own fashion.

"What kind of a love it was—of what value—I cannot tell you. I do not think it was very high in the scale. Only he felt it for me, and for no other woman I believe.

472

"It never was a love that I could entirely understand or respect; yet,—it is odd but true—I cared something for it—perhaps because, in spite of its unfamiliar and sometimes repellent disguises—it *was* love after all.

"And now, as at heart and in mind you and I are one; and as I keep nothing of real importance from you —perhaps *can* not; I must tell you that José Querida came that day to ask me to marry him.

"I tried to make him understand that I could not think of such a thing; and he lost his head and became violent. That is how the table fell:—I had started toward the door when he sprang back to block me, and the low window-sill caught him under the knees, and he fell outward into the yard.

"I know of course that no blame could rest on me, but it was a terrible and dreadful thing that happened there in one brief second; and somehow it seems to have moved in me depths that have never before been stirred.

"The newspapers, as you know, published it merely as an accident—which it really was. But they might have made it, by innuendo, a horror for me. However, they put it so simply and so unsuspiciously that José Querida might have been any nice man calling on any nice woman.

"Louis, I have never been so lonely in my life as I have been since José Querida died; alas! not because he has gone out of my life forever, but because, somehow, the manner of his death has made me realise how difficult it is for a woman alone to contend with men in a man's own world.

"Do what she may to maintain her freedom, her integrity, there is always,—sometimes impalpable, sometimes not—a steady, remorseless pressure on her, forcing her unwillingly to take frightened cognisance of men;—take into account their inexorable desire for domination; the subtle cohesion existent among them which, at moments, becomes like a wall of adamant barring, limiting, inclosing and forcing women toward the deep-worn grooves which women have trodden through the sad centuries;—and which they tread still—and will tread perhaps for years to come before the real enfranchisement of mankind begins.

"I do not mean to write bitterly, dear; but, somehow, all this seems to bear significantly, ominously, upon my situation in the world.

"When I first knew you I felt so young, so confident, so free, so scornful of custom, so wholesomely emancipated from silly and unjust conventions, that perhaps I overestimated my own vigour and ability to go my way, unvexed, unfettered in this man's world, and let the world make its own journey in peace. But it will not.

"Twice, now, within a month,—and not through any conscious fault of mine—this man's world has shown its teeth at me; I have been menaced by its innate scorn of woman, and have, by chance, escaped a publicity which would have damned me so utterly that I would not have cared to live.

"And dear, for the first time I really begin to understand now what the shelter of a family means; what it is to have law on my side,—and a man who understands his man's world well enough to fight it with its own weapons;—well enough to protect a woman from things she never dreamed might menace her.

"When that policeman came into my room,—dear,

474

you will think me a perfect coward—but suddenly I seemed to realise what law meant, and that it had power to protect me or destroy me. . . . And I was frightened,—and the table lay there with the fragments of broken china—and there was that dreadful window—and I—I who knew how he died!—Louis! Louis! guiltless as I was,—blameless in thought and deed—I died a thousand deaths there while the big policeman and the reporters were questioning me.

"If it had not been for what José was generous enough to say, I could never have thought out a lie to tell them; I should have told them how it had really happened. . . . And what the papers would have printed about him and about me, God only knows.

"Never, never had I needed you as I needed you at that moment. . . . Well; I lied to them, somehow; I said to them what José had said—that he was seated on the window-ledge, lost his balance, clutched at the table, overturned it, and fell. And they believed me. . . . It is the first lie since I was a little child, that I have ever knowingly told. . . . And I know now that I could never contrive to tell another.

"Dear, let me try to think out what is best for us. . . . And forgive me, Louis, if I can not help a thought or two of self creeping in. I am so terribly alone. Somehow I am beginning to believe that it may sometimes be a weakness to totally ignore one's self. . . . Not that I consider myself of importance compared to you, my darling; not that I would fail to set aside any thought of self where your welfare is concerned. You know that, don't you?

"But I have been wondering how it would be with you if I passed quietly and absolutely out of your life.

That is what I am trying to determine. Because it must be either that or the tie unrecognised by civilisation. And which would be better for you? I do not know yet. I ask more time. Don't write me. Your silence will accord it.

"You are always in my thoughts.

"VALERIE."

Ogilvy came into the studio that afternoon, loquacious, in excellent humour, and lighting a pipe, detailed what news he had while Neville tried to hide his own deep perplexity and anxiety under a cordial welcome.

"You know," said Ogilvy, "that all the time you've given me and all your kindness and encouragement has made a corker of that picture of mine."

"You did it yourself," said Neville. "It's good work, Sam."

"Sure it's good work—being mostly yours. And what do you think, Kelly; it's sold!"

"Good for you!"

"Certainly it's good for me. I need the mazuma. A courteous multi purchased it for his Long Branch cottage—said cottage costing a million. What?"

"Oh, you're doing very well," laughed Neville.

"I've *got* to. . . . I've—h'm!—undertaken to assume obligations toward civilisation—h'm!—and certain duties to my—h'm—country———"

"What on earth are you driving at?" asked Neville, eying him.

"Huh! Driving single just at present; practising for tandem—h'm!—and a spike—h'm—some day—I hope—of course———"

" Sam ! "

" Hey? "

" Are you trying to say something? "

" Oh, Lord, no! Why, Kelly, did you suspect that I was really attempting to convey anything to you which I was really too damned embarrassed to tell you in the patois of my native city? "

" It sounded that way," observed Neville, smiling.

" Did it? " Ogilvy considered, head on one side. " Did it sound anything like a—h'm!—a man who was trying to—h'm!—to tell you that he was going to—h'm!—to try to get somebody to try to let him try to tell her that he wanted to—marry her? "

" Good heavens! " exclaimed Neville, bewildered, " what. do you mean? "

Ogilvy pirouetted, picked up a mahl-stick, and began a lively fencing bout with an imaginary adversary.

" I'm going to get married," he said amiably.

" What! "

" Sure."

" To whom? "

" To Hélène d'Enver. Only she doesn't know it yet."

" What an infernal idiot you are, Sam! "

" Ya-as, so they say. Some say I'm an ass, others a bally idiot, others merely refer to me as imbecile. And so it goes, Kelly,—so it goes."

He flourished his mahl-stick, neatly punctured the air, and cried " Hah! " very fiercely.

Then he said:

" I've concluded to let Hélène know about it this afternoon."

" About what?—you monkey? "

"About our marriage. *Won't* it surprise her though! Oh, no! But I think I'll let her into the secret before some suspicious gink gets wind of it and tells her himself."

Neville looked at the boy, perplexed, undecided, until he caught his eye. And over Sam's countenance stole a vivid and beauteous blush.

"Sam! I—upon my word I believe you mean it!"

"Sure I do!"

Neville grasped his hand:

"My dear fellow!" he said cordially, "I was slow, not unsympathetic. I'm frightfully glad—I'm perfectly delighted. She's a charming and sincere woman. Go in and win and God bless you both!"

Ogilvy wrung his hand, then, to relieve his feelings, ran all over the floor like a spider and was pretending to spin a huge web in a corner when Harry Annan and Rita Tevis came in and discovered him.

"Hah!" he exclaimed, "flies! Two nice, silly, appetising flies. Pretend to fall into my web, Rita, and begin to buzz like mad!"

Rita's dainty nose went up into the air, but Annan succumbed to the alluring suggestion, and presently he was buzzing frantically in a corner while Sam spun an imaginary web all over him.

Rita and Neville looked on for a while.

"Sam never will grow up," she said disdainfully.

"He's fortunate," observed Neville.

"*You* don't think so."

"I wish I knew what I did think, Rita. How is John?"

"I came to tell you. He has gone to Dartford."

"To see Dr. Ogilvy? Good! I'm glad, Rita.

"Ogilvy . . . began a lively fencing bout with an imaginary
adversary."

Billy Ogilvy usually makes people do what he tells them
to do."

The girl stood silent, eyes lowered. After a while
she looked up at him; and in her unfaltering but sorrowful gaze he read the tragedy which he had long since
suspected.

Neither spoke for a moment; he held out both

hands; she laid her's in them, and her gaze became remote.

After a while she said in a low voice:

"Let me be with you now and then while he's
away; will you, Kelly?"

"Yes. Would you like to pose for me? I haven't
anything pressing on hand. You might begin now if
it suits you."

"May I?" she asked gratefully.

"Of course, child. . . . Let me think—" He looked
again into her dark blue eyes, absently, then suddenly
his attention became riveted upon something which he
seemed to be reading in her face.

Long before Sam and Harry had ended their
puppy-like scuffling and had retired to woo their respective deputy-muses, Rita was seated on the model-
stand, and Neville had already begun that strange and
sombre picture afterward so famous, and about which
one of the finest of our modern poets wrote:

"Her gold hair, fallen about her face
    Made light within that shadowy place,
        But on her garments lay the dust
    Of many a vanished race.

"Her deep eyes, gazing straight ahead,
    Saw years and days and hours long dead,
        While strange gems glittered at her feet,
    Yellow, and green, and red.

"And ever from the shadows came
    Voices to pierce her heart like flame,
        The great bats fanned her with their wings,
    The voices called her name.

480

"But yet her look turned not aside
From the black deep where dreams abide,
    Where worlds and pageantries lay dead
Beneath that viewless tide.

"Her elbow on her knee was set,
Her strong hand propt her chin, and yet
    No man might name that look she wore,
Nor any man forget."

All day long in the pleasant June weather they
worked together over the picture; and if he really knew
what he was about, it is uncertain, for his thoughts were
of Valerie; and he painted as in a dream, and with a
shadowy splendour that seemed even to him unreal.

They scarcely spoke; now and then Rita came silently on sandalled feet to stand behind him and look at
what he had done.

The first time she thought to herself, "Querida!"
But the second time she remained mute; and when the
daylight was waning to a golden gloom in the room she
came a third time and stood with one hand on his arm,
her eyes fixed upon the dawning mystery on the canvas
—spellbound under the sombre magnificence already
vaguely shadowed forth from infinite depth of shade.

Gladys came and rubbed and purred around his
legs; the most recent progeny toddled after her, ratty
tails erect; sportive, casual little optimists frisking unsteadily on wavering legs among the fading sunbeams
on the floor.

The sunbeams died out on wall and ceiling; high
through the glass roof above, a shoal of rosy clouds
paled to saffron, then to a cinder gray. And the first
night-hawk, like a huge, erratic swallow, sailed into view,

soaring, tumbling aloft, while its short raucous cry
sounded incessantly above the roofs and chimneys.

Neville was still seated before his canvas, palette flat
across his left arm, the sheaf of wet brushes held loosely.

" I suppose you are dining with Valerie," he said.

" No."

He turned and looked at her, inquiringly.

" Valerie has gone away."

" Where? "

" I don't know, Kelly. . . . I was not to know."

" I see." He picked up a handful of waste and
slowly began to clean the brushes, one by one. Then
he drove them deep into a bowl of black soap.

" Shall we dine together here, Rita? "

" If you care to have me."

" Yes, I do."

He laid aside his palette, rang up the kitchen, gave
his order, and slowly returned to where Rita was seated.

Dinner was rather a silent affair. They touched
briefly and formally on Querida and his ripening talent
prematurely annihilated; they spoke of men they knew
who were to come after him—a long, long way after
him.

" I don't know who is to take his place," mused
Neville over his claret.

" You."

" Not his place, Rita. He thought so; but that
place must remain his."

" Perhaps. But you are carving out your own
niche in a higher tier. You are already beginning to
do it; and yesterday his niche was the higher. . . .
Yet, after all—after all——"

He nodded. " Yes," he said, " what does it matter

"Then Rita came silently on sandalled feet to stand behind him
and look at what he had done."

to him, now? A man carves out his resting place as
you say, but he carves it out in vain. Those who come
after him will either place him in his proper sepulchre
. . . or utterly neglect him. . . . And neglect or transfer will cause him neither happiness nor pain. . . .
Both are ended for Querida;—let men exalt him above
all, or bury him and his work out of sight—what does
he care about it now? He has had all that life held for

him, and what another life may promise him no man can know. All reward for labour is here, Rita; and the reward lasts only while the pleasure in labour lasts. Creative work—even if well done—loses its savour when it is finished. Happiness in it ends with the final touch. It is like a dead thing to him who created it; men's praise or blame makes little impression; and the aftertaste of both is either bitter or flat and lasts but a moment."

"Are you a little morbid, Kelly?"

"Am I?"

"It seems to me so."

"And you, Rita?"

She shook her pretty head in silence.

After a while Gladys jumped up into her lap, and she lay back in her arm-chair smoothing the creature's fur, and gazing absently into space.

"Kelly," she said, "how many, many years ago it seems when you came up to Delaware County to see us."

"It seems very long ago to me, too."

She lifted her blue eyes:

"May I speak plainly? I have known you a long while. There is only one man I like better. But there is no woman in the world whom I love as I love Valerie West. . . . May I speak plainly?"

"Yes."

"Then—be fair to her, Kelly. Will you?"

"I will try."

"Try very hard. For after all it *is* a man's world, and she doesn't understand it. Try to be fair to her, Kelly. For—whether or not the laws that govern the world are man-made and unjust—they are, nevertheless, the only laws. Few men can successfully fight them;

484

no woman can—yet. . . . I am not angering you, am I? "

" No. Go on."

" I have so little to say—I who feel so deeply—deeply. . . . And the laws are always there, Kelly, always there—fair or unfair, just or unjust—they are always there to govern the world that framed them. And a woman disobeys them at her peril."

She moved slightly in her chair and sat supporting her head on one pretty ringless hand.

" Yet," she said, " although a woman disobeys any law at her peril—laws which a man may often ignore with impunity—there is one law to which no woman should dare subscribe. And it is sometimes known as ' The Common Law of Marriage.' "

She sat silent for a while, her gaze never leaving his shadowy face.

" That is the only law—if it is truly a law—that a woman must ignore. All others it is best for her to observe. And if the laws of marriage are merely man-made or divine, I do not know. There is a din in the world to-day which drowns the voices preaching old beliefs. . . . And a girl is deafened by the clamour. . . . And I don't know.

" But, it seems to me, that back of the laws men have made—if there be nothing divine in their inspiration—there is another foundation solid enough to carry them. Because it seems to me that the world's laws—even when unjust—are built on natural laws. And how can a girl say that these natural laws are unjust because they have fashioned her to bear children and feed them from her own body?

" And another thing, Kelly; if a man breaks a man-

made law—founded, we believe, on a divine command-
ment—he suffers only in a spiritual and moral sense.
. .. . And with us it may be more than that. For
women, at least, hell is on earth."

He stirred in his chair, and his sombre gaze rested
on the floor at her feet.

"What are we to do?" he said dully.

Rita shook her head:

"I don't know. I am not instructing you, Kelly,
only recalling to your mind what you already know;
what all men know, and find so convenient to forget.
Love is not excuse enough; the peril is unequally divided. The chances are uneven; the odds are unfair.
If a man really loves a woman, how can he hazard her
in a game of chance that is not square? How can he
let her offer more than he has at stake—even if she is
willing? How can he permit her to risk more than he
is even able to risk? How can he accept a magnanimity
which leaves him her hopeless debtor? But men have
done it, men will continue to do it; God alone knows
how they reconcile it with their manhood or find it in
their hearts to deal so unfairly by us. But they do.
. . . And still we stake all; and proudly overlook the
chances against us; and face the contemptible odds
with a smile, dauntless and—damned!"

He leaned forward in the dusk; she could see his
bloodless features now only as a pale blot in the twilight.

"All this I knew, Rita. But it is just as well, perhaps, that you remind me."

"I thought it might be as well. The world has
grown very clever; but after all there is no steadier
anchor for a soul than a platitude."

486

Ogilvy and Annan came mincing in about nine o'clock, disposed for flippancy and gossip; but neither Neville nor Rita encouraged them; so after a while they took their unimpaired cheerfulness and horse-play elsewhere, leaving the two occupants of the studio to their own silent devices.

It was nearly midnight when he walked back with Rita to her rooms.

And now day followed day in a sequence of limpid dawns and cloudless sunsets. Summer began with a clear, hot week in June, followed by three days' steady downpour which freshened and cooled the city and unfolded, in square and park, everything green into magnificent maturity.

Every day Neville and Rita worked together in the studio; and every evening they walked together in the park or sat in the cool, dusky studio, companionably conversational or permitting silence to act as their interpreter.

Then John Burleson came back from Dartford after remaining there ten days under Dr. Ogilvy's observation; and Rita arrived at the studio next day almost smiling.

"We're going to Arizona," she said. "*What* do you think of that, Kelly?"

"You poor child!" exclaimed Neville, taking her hands into his and holding them closely.

"Why, Kelly," she said gently, "I knew he had to go. This has not taken me unawares."

"I hoped there might be some doubt," he said.

"There was none in my mind. I foresaw it. Listen to me: twice in a woman's life a woman becomes a prophetess. That fatal clairvoyance is permitted to a woman twice in her life—and the second time it is neither for herself that she foresees the future, nor for him whom she loves. . . . "

"I wish—I wish—" he hesitated; and she flushed brightly.

"I know what you wish, Kelly dear. I don't think it will ever happen. But it is so much for me to be permitted to remain near him—so much!—Ah, you don't know, Kelly! You don't know!"

"Would you marry him?"

Her honest blue eyes met his:

"If he asked me; and if he still wished it—after he knew."

"Could you ever be less to him—and perhaps more, Rita?"

"Do you mean——"

He nodded deliberately.

She hung her head.

"Yes," she said, "if I could be no more I would be what I could."

"And you tell *me* that, after all that you have said?"

"I did not pretend to speak for men, Kelly. I told you that women had, and women still would overlook the chances menacing them and face the odds dauntlessly. . . . Because, whatever a man is—if a woman loves him enough—he is worth to her what she gives."

·"Rita! Rita! Is it *you* who content yourself with such sorry philosophy?"

"Yes, it is I. You asked me and I answer you. Whatever I said—I know only one thing now. And you know what that is."

"And where am I to look for sympathy and support in my own decision? What can I think now about all that you have said to me?"

"You will never forget it, Kelly—whatever becomes of the girl who said it. Because it's the truth, no matter whose lips uttered it."

He released her hands and she went away to dress herself for the pose. When she returned and seated herself he picked up his palette and brushes and began in silence.

That evening he went to see John Burleson and found him smoking tranquilly in the midst of disorder. Packing cases, trunks, bundles, boxes were scattered and piled up in every direction, and the master of the establishment, apparently in excellent health, reclined on a lounge in the centre of chaos, the long clay stem of a church-warden pipe between his lips, puffing rings at the ceiling.

"Hello, Kelly!" he exclaimed, sitting up; "I've got to move out of this place. Rita told you all about it, didn't she? Isn't it rotten hard luck?"

"Not a bit of it. What did Billy Ogilvy say?"

"Oh, I've got *it* all right. Not seriously yet. What's Arizona like, anyway?"

"Half hell, half paradise, they say."

"Then me for the celestial section. Ogilvy gave me the name of a place"—he fumbled about—"Rita has it, I believe. . . . Isn't she a corker to go? My conscience, Kelly, what a Godsend it will be to have a Massachusetts girl out there to talk to!"

"Isn't she going as your model?"

"My Lord, man! Don't you talk to a model? Is

489

a nice girl who poses for a fellow anything extra-human or superhuman or—or unhuman or inhuman—so that intelligent conversation becomes impossible? "

" No," began Neville, laughing, but Burleson interrupted excitedly:

" A girl can be anything she chooses if she's all right, can't she? And Rita comes from Massachusetts, doesn't she? "

" Certainly."

" Not only from Massachusetts, but from Hitherford!" added Burleson triumphantly. " *I* came from Hitherford. My grandfather knew hers. Why, man alive, Rita Tevis is entitled to do anything she chooses to do."

" That's one way of looking at it, anyway," admitted Neville gravely.

" I look at it that way. *You* can't; you're not from Massachusetts; but you have a sort of a New England name, too. It's Yankee, isn't it? "

" Southern."

" Oh," said Burleson, honestly depressed; " I *am* sorry. There were Nevilles in Hitherford Lower Falls two hundred years ago. I've always liked to think of you as originating, somehow or other, in Massachusetts Bay."

" No, John; unlike McGinty, I am unfamiliar with the cod-thronged ocean deeps. . . . When are you going? "

" Day after to-morrow. Rita says you don't need her any longer on that picture——"

" Lord, man! If I did I wouldn't hold you up. But don't worry, John; she wouldn't let me. . . . She's a fine specimen of girl," he added casually.

490

" Do you suppose that is news to me? "

" Oh, no; I'm sure you find her amusing——"

" What! "

" Amusing," repeated Neville innocently. " Don't you? "

" That is scarcely the word I would have chosen, Kelly. I have a very warm admiration and a very sincere respect for Rita Tevis——"

" John! You sound like a Puritan making love! "

Burleson was intensely annoyed:

" You'd better understand, Kelly, that Rita Tevis is as well born as I am, and that there would be nothing at all incongruous in any declaration that any decent man might make her! "

" Why, I know that. "

" I'm glad you do. And I'm gratified that what you said has given me the opportunity to make myself very plain on the subject of Rita Tevis. It may amaze you to know that her great grandsire carried a flintlock with the Hitherford Minute Men, and fell most respectably at Boston Neck."

" Certainly, John. I knew she was all right. But I wasn't sure you knew it——"

" Confound it! Of course I did. I've always known it. Do you think I'd care for her so much if she wasn't all right? "

Neville smiled at him gravely, then held out his hand:

" Give my love to her, John. I'll see you both again before you go."

For nearly two weeks he had not heard a word from Valerie West. Rita and John Burleson had departed, cheerful, sure of early convalescence and a complete and radical cure.

Neville went with them to the train, but his mind was full of his own troubles and he could scarcely keep his attention on the ponderous conversation of Burleson, who was admonishing him and Ogilvy impartially concerning the true interpretation of creative art.

He turned aside to Rita when opportunity offered and said in a low voice:

" Before you go, tell me where Valerie is."

" I can't, Kelly."

" Did you promise her not to? "

" Yes."

He said, slowly: " I haven't had one word from her. in nearly two weeks. Is she well? "

" Yes. She came into town this morning to say good-bye to me."

" I didn't know she was out of town," he said, troubled.

" She has been, and is now. That's all I can tell you, Kelly dear."

" She *is* coming back, isn't she? "

" I hope so."

" Don't you know? "

She looked into his anxious and miserable face and gently shook her head:

" I *don't* know, Kelly."

" Didn't she say—intimate anything——"

" No. . . . I don't think she knows—yet."

He said, very quietly: " If she ever comes to any conclusion that it is better for us both never to meet again—I might be as dead as Querida for any work I should ever again set hand to.

"If she will not marry me, but will let things remain as they are, at least I can go on caring for her and working out this miserable problem of life. But if she goes out of my life, life will go out of me. I know that now."

Rita looked at him pitifully:

"Valerie's mind is her own, Kelly. It is the most honest mind I have ever known; and nothing on earth— no pain that her decision might inflict upon her— would swerve it a hair's breath from what she concludes is the right thing to do."

"I know it," he said, swallowing a sudden throb of fear.

"Then what can I say to you?"

"Nothing. I must wait."

"Kelly, if you loved her enough you would not even wait."

"What!"

"Because her return to you will mean only one thing. Are you going to accept it of her?"

"What can I do? I can't live without her!"

"*Her* problem is nobler, Kelly. She is asking herself not whether she can live life through without *you* —but whether you can live life well, and to the full, without *her?*"

Neville flushed painfully.

"Yes," he said, "*that* is Valerie. I'm not worth the anxiety, the sorrow that I have brought her. I'm not worth marrying; and I'm not worth a heavier sacrifice. . . . I'm trying to think less of myself, Rita, and more of her. . . . Perhaps, if I knew she were happy, I could stand—losing her. . . . If she could be—without me—" He checked himself, for the struggle was unnerving him; then he set his face firmly and looked straight at Rita.

"Do you believe she could forget me and be contented and tranquil—if I gave her the chance?"

"Are *you* talking of self-sacrifice for *her* sake?"

He drew a deep, uneven breath:

"I—suppose it's—that."

"You mean that you're willing to eliminate yourself and give her an opportunity to see a little of the world—a little of its order and tranquillity and quieter happiness?—a chance to meet interesting women and attractive men of her own age—as she is certain to do through her intimacy with the Countess d'Enver?"

"Yes," he said, "that is what must be done. . . . I've been blind—and rottenly selfish. I did not mean to be. . . . I've tried to force her—I have done nothing else since I fell in love with her, but force her toward people whom she has a perfect right not to care for— even if they happen to be my own people. She has felt nothing but a steady and stupid pressure from me;— heard from me nothing except importunities—the merciless, obstinate urging of my own views—which, God forgive me, I thought were the only views because they were respectable!"

He stood, head lowered, nervously clenching and unclenching his hands.

"It was not for her own sake—that's the worst of it! It was for my sake—because I've had respectability inculcated until I can't conceive of my doing anything not respectable. . . . Once, something else got away with me—and I gave it rein for a moment—until checked. . . . I'm really no different from other men."

"I think you are beginning to be, Kelly."

"Am I? I don't know. But the worst of it was my selfishness—my fixed idea that her marrying me was the *only* salvation for her. . . . I never thought of giving her a chance of seeing other people—other men—better men—of seeing a tranquil, well-ordered world—of being in it and of it. I behaved as though my world—the fragment inhabited by my friends and family—was the only alternative to this one. I've been a fool, Rita; and a cruel one."

"No, only an average man, Kelly. . . . If I give you Valerie's address, would you write and give her her freedom—for her own sake?—the freedom to try life in that well-ordered world we speak of? . . . Because she is very young. Life is all before her. Who can foretell what friends she may be destined to make; what opportunities she may have. I care a great deal for you, Kelly; but I love Valerie. . . . And, there *are* other men in the world after all;—but there is only one Valerie. . . . And—*how truly do you love her?*"

"Enough," he said under his breath.

"Enough to—leave her alone?"

"Yes."

"Then write and tell her so. Here is the address."

She slipped a small bit of folded paper into Neville's hand.

"We must join the others, now," she said calmly.

Annan had come up, and he and Ogilvy were noisily baiting Burleson amid shouts of laughter and a protesting roar from John.

"Stop it, you wretches," said Rita amiably, entering the little group. "John, are you never going to learn not to pay any attention to this pair of infants?"

"Are you going to kiss me good-bye, Rita, when the train departs?" inquired Sam, anxiously.

"Certainly; I kissed Gladys good-bye——"

"Before all this waiting room full of people?" persisted Sam. "*Are* you?"

"Why I'll do it now if you like, Sammy dear."

"They'll take you for my sister," said Sam, disgusted.

"Or your nurse; John, what *is* that man bellowing through the megaphone?"

"Our train," said Burleson, picking up the satchels. He dropped them again to shake the hands that were offered:

"Good-bye, John, dear old fellow! You'll get all over this thing in a jiffy out there. You'll be back in no time at all! Don't worry, and get well!"

He smiled confidently and shook all their hands. Rita's pretty face was pale; she let Ogilvy kiss her cheek, shook hands with Annan, and then, turning to Neville, put both hands on his shoulders and kissed him on the mouth.

"Give her her chance, Kelly," she whispered. . . . "And it shall be rendered unto you seven-fold."

"No, Rita; it never will be now."

"Who knows?"

"Rita! Rita!" he said under his breath, "where I am ending, she must begin. . . . You are right: the world needs her. Try as I might, I never could be worth what she is worth without effort. It is my life which does not matter, not hers. I will do what ought to be done. Don't be afraid. I will do it. And thank God that it is not too late."

That night, seated at his desk in the studio, he looked at the calendar. It was the thirteenth day since he had heard from her; the last day but two of the fifteen days she had asked for. The day after to-morrow she would have come, or would have written him that she was renouncing him forever for his own sake. Which might it have been? He would never know now.

He wrote her:

"Dearest of women, Rita has been loyal to you. It was only when I explained to her for what purpose I wished your address that she wisely gave it to me.

"Dearest, from the beginning of our acquaintance and afterward when it ripened into friendship and finally became love, upon you has rested the burden of decision; and I have permitted it.

"Even now, as I am writing here in the studio, the burden lies heavily upon your girl's shoulders and is weighting your girl's heart. And it must not be so any longer.

"I have never, perhaps, really meant to be selfish; a man in love really doesn't know what he means. But now I know what I have done; and what must be undone.

"You were perfectly right. It was for you to say whether you would marry me or not. It was for you to decide whether it was possible or impossible for you to appear as my wife in a world in which you had had no experience. It was for you to generously decide whether a rupture between that world and myself—between my family and myself—would render me—and yourself—eternally unhappy.

"You were free to decide; you used your own in-

499

tellect, and you so decided. And I had no right to question you—I have no right now. I shall never question you again.

"Then, because you loved me, and because it was the kind of love that ignored self, you offered me a supreme sacrifice. And I did not refuse; I merely continued to fight for what I thought ought to be—distressing, confusing, paining you with the stupid, obstinate reiterations of my importunities. And you stood fast by your colours.

"Dear, I *was* wrong. And so were you. Those were not the only alternatives. I allowed them to appear so because of selfishness. . . . Alas, Valerie, in spite of all I have protested and professed of love and passion for you, to-day, for the first time, have I really loved you enough to consider you, alone. And with God's help I will do so always.

"You have offered me two alternatives: to give yourself and your life to me without marriage; or to quietly slip out of my life forever.

"And it never occurred to you—and I say, with shame, that it never occurred to me—that I might quietly efface myself and my demands from *your* life; leave you free and at peace to rest and develop in that new and quieter world which your beauty and goodness has opened to you.

"Desirable people have met you more than half-way, and they like you. Your little friend, Hélène d'Enver, is a genuine and charming woman. Your friendship for her will mean all that you have so far missed in life; all that a girl is entitled to.

"Through her you will widen the circle of your acquaintances and form newer and better friendships.

500

You will meet men and women of your own age and your own tastes which is what ought to happen.

"And it is right and just and fair that you enter into the beginning of your future with a mind unvexed and a heart untroubled by conflicts which can never solve for you and me any future life together.

"I do not believe you will ever forget me, or wish to, wholly. Time heals—otherwise the world had gone mad some centuries ago.

"But whatever destiny is reserved for you, I know you will meet it with the tranquillity and the sweet courage which you have always shown.

"What kind of future I wish for you, I need not write here. You know. And it is for the sake of that future—for the sake of the girl whose unselfish life has at last taught me and shamed me, that I give you up forever.

"Dear, perhaps you had better not answer this for a long, long time. Then, when that clever surgeon, Time, has effaced all scars—and when not only tranquillity is yours but, perhaps, a deeper happiness is in sight, write and tell me so. And the great god Kelly, nodding before his easel, will rouse up from his Olympian revery and totter away to find a sheaf of blessings to bestow upon the finest, truest, and loveliest girl in all the world.

"*Halcyonii dies! Fortem posce animum! Forsan et haec olim meminisse juvabit. Vale!*

"Louis Neville."

CHAPTER XVII

THE fifteenth day of her absence had come and gone and there had been no word from her.

Whether or not he had permitted himself to expect any, the suspense had been none the less almost unendurable. He walked the floor of the studio all day long, scarcely knowing what he was about, insensible to fatigue or to anything except the dull, ceaseless beating of his heart. He seemed older, thinner—a man whose sands were running very swiftly.

With the dawn of the fifteenth day of her absence a gray pallor had come into his face; and it remained there. Ogilvy and Annan sauntered into the studio to visit him, twice, and the second time they arrived bearing gifts—favourite tonics, prescriptions, and pills.

" You look like hell, Kelly," observed Sam with tactful and characteristic frankness. " Try a few of this assorted dope. Harry and I dote on dope:

> "'*After the bat is over,*
> *After the last cent's spent,*
> *And the pigs have gone from the clover*
> *And the very last gent has went;*
> *After the cards are scattered,*
> *After I've paid the bill,*
> *Weary and rocky and battered*
> *I swallow my liver pill!*'"

—he sang, waltzing slowly around the room with Annan until, inadvertently, they stepped upon the tail of Gladys who went off like a pack of wet fire-crackers; whereupon they retired in confusion to their respective abodes above.

Evening came, and with evening, letters; but none from her. And slowly the stealthy twilight hours dragged their heavy minutes toward darkness; and night crawled into the room like some sinister living thing, and found him still pacing the floor.

Through the dusky June silence far below in the street sounded the clatter of wheels; but they never stopped before his abode. Voices rose faintly at moments in the still air, borne upward as from infinite depths; but her voice would never sound again for him: he knew it now—never again for him. And yet he paced the floor, listening. The pain in his heart grew duller at intervals, benumbed by the tension; but it always returned, sickening him, almost crazing him.

Late in the evening he gave way under the torture —turned coward, and started to write to her. Twice he began letters—pleading with her to forget his letter; begging her to come back. And destroyed them with hands that shook like the hands of a sick man. Then the dull insensibility to pain gave him a little respite. But later the misery and terror of it drove him out into the street with an insane idea of seeking her—of taking the train and finding her.

He throttled that impulse; the struggle exhausted him; and he returned, listlessly, to the door and stood there, vacant-eyed, staring into the lamp-lit street.

Once he caught sight of a shadowy, graceful figure crossing the avenue—a lithe young silhouette against the gas-light—and his heart stood still for an instant: but it was not she, and he swayed where he stood, under the agony of reaction, dazed by the rushing recession of emotion.

Then a sudden fear seized him that she might have come while he had been away. He had been as far as the avenue. Could she have come?

But when he arrived at his door he had scarce courage enough to go in. She had a key; she might have entered. Had she entered: was she there, behind that closed door? To go in and find the studio empty seemed almost more than he could endure. But, at last, he went in; and he found the studio empty.

Confused, shaken, tortured, he began again his aimless tour of the place, ranging the four walls like a wild creature dulled to insanity by long imprisonment—passing backward, forward, to and fro, across, around, his footsteps timing the dreadful monotone of his heart, his pulse beating, thudding out his doom.

She would never come; never come again. She had determined what was best to do; she had arrived at her decision. Perhaps his letter had convinced her,—had cleared her vision;—the letter which he had been mad enough to write—fool enough—God!—perhaps brave enough. . . . But if what he had done in his madness was bravery, it was an accursed thing; and he set his teeth and cursed himself scarce knowing what he was saying.

It promised to be an endless night for him; and there were other nights to come—interminable nights. And now he began to watch the clock—strained eyes riveted on the stiff gilded hands—and on the little one, jerkily, pitilessly recording the seconds and twitching them one by one into eternity.

Nearer and nearer to midnight crept the gilded, flamboyant hour-hand; the gaunter minute-hand was slowly but inexorably overtaking it. Nearer, nearer, they drew together; then came the ominous click; a moment's suspense; the high-keyed gong quivered twelve times under the impact of the tiny steel hammer.

And he never would hear her voice again. And he dropped to his knees asking mercy on them both.

In his dulled ears still lingered the treble ringing echo of the bell—lingered, reiterated, repeated incessantly, until he thought he was going mad. Then, of a sudden, he realised that the telephone was ringing; and he reeled from his knees to his feet, and crept forward into the shadows, feeling his way like a blind man.

"Louis?"

But he could not utter a sound.

"Louis, is it you?"

"Yes," he whispered.

"What is the matter? Are you ill? Your voice is so strange. *Are* you?"

"No!—Is it *you*, Valerie?"

"You know it is!"

"Where—are you?"

"In my room—where I have been all day."

"You have been—*there!* You have been *here*— in this city—all this time——"

"I came in on the morning train. I wanted to be sure. There *have* been such things as railroad delays you know."

"Why—*why* didn't you let me know——"

"Louis! You will please to recollect that I had until midnight . . . I—was busy. Besides, midnight has just sounded—and here I am."

17   505

He waited.

"I received your letter." Her voice had the sweet, familiar, rising inflection which seemed to invite an answer.

"Yes," he muttered, "I wrote to you."

"Do you wish to know what I thought of your letter?"

"Yes," he breathed.

"I will tell you some other time; not now. . . . Have you been perfectly well, Louis? But I heard all about you, every day,—through Rita. Do you know I am quite mad to see that picture you painted of her, —the new one—'Womanhood.' She says it is a great picture—really great. Is it?"

He did not answer.

"Louis!"

"Yes."

"I would like to see that picture."

"Valerie?"

"Yes?"—sweetly impatient.

"Are we to see each other again?"

She said calmly: "I didn't ask to see *you*, Louis; I asked to see a picture which you recently painted, called 'Womanhood.'"

He remained silent and presently she called him again by name: "You say that you are well —or rather Rita said so two days ago—and I'm wondering whether in the interim you've fallen ill? Two days without news from you is rather disquieting. Please tell me at once exactly how you are?"

He succeeded in forcing something resembling a laugh: "I am all right," he said.

" I don't see how you could be—after the letter you wrote me.   How much of it did you mean? "

He was silent.

" Louis!   Answer me! "

" All—of it," he managed to reply.

"She knelt down beside the bed and . . . said whatever prayer she
had in mind."

" *All!* "

" Yes."

" Then—perhaps you scarcely expected me to call you up to-night.   Did you? "

" No."

" Suppose I had not done so."

He shivered slightly, but remained mute.

" Answer me, Louis? "

" It would have been—better."

" For you? "

" For—both."

" Do you believe it? "

" Yes."

" Then—have I any choice except to say—good-night? "

" No choice. Good-night."

" Good-night."

He crept, shaking, into his bed-room, sat down, resting his hands on his knees and staring at vacancy.

Valerie, in her room, hung up the receiver, buried her face in her hands for a moment, then quietly turned, lowering her hands from her face, and looked down at the delicate, intimate garments spread in order on the counterpane beside her. There was a new summer gown there, too—a light, dainty, fragile affair on which she had worked while away. Beside it lay a big summer hat of white straw and white lilacs.

She stood for a moment, reflecting; then she knelt down beside the bed and covered her eyes again while she said whatever prayer she had in mind.

It was not a very short petition, because it concerned Neville. She asked nothing for herself except as it regarded him or might matter to his peace of mind. Otherwise what she said, asked, and offered, related wholly to Neville.

Presently she rose and went lightly and silently

about her ablutions; and afterward she dressed herself in the fragile snowy garments ranged so methodically upon the white counterpane, each in its proper place.

She was longer over her hair, letting it fall in a dark lustrous cloud to her waist, then combing and gathering it and bringing it under discipline.

She put on her gown, managing somehow to fasten it, her lithe young body and slender arms aiding her to achieve the impossible between neck and shoulders. Afterward she pinned on her big white hat.

At the door she paused for a second; took a last look at the quiet, white little room tranquil and silent in the lamplight; then she turned off the light and went out, softly, holding in her hands a key which fitted no door of her own.

One o'clock sounded heavily from Saint Hilda's as she left her house; the half hour was striking as she stooped in the dark hallway outside the studio and fitted the key she held—the key that was to unlock for her the mystery of the world.

He had not heard her. She groped her way into the unlighted studio, touched with caressing finger-tips the vague familiar shapes that the starlight, falling through the glass above, revealed to her as she passed.

In the little inner room she paused. There was a light through the passageway beyond, but she stood here a moment, looking around her while memories of the place deepened the colour in her cheeks.

Then she went forward, timidly, and stood at his closed door, listening.

A sudden fright seized her; one hand flew to her breast, her throat—covered her eyes for a moment—and fell limp by her side.

"She was longer over her hair . . . gathering it and bringing it under discipline."

"Louis!" she faltered. She heard him spring to his feet and stand as though transfixed.

"Louis," she said, "it is I. Will you open your door to me?"

The sudden flood of electric light dazzled her; then she saw him standing there, one hand still resting on the door knob.

"I've come," she said, with a faint smile.

"Valerie! My God!"

She stood, half smiling, half fearful, her dark eyes meeting his, two friendly little hands outstretched. Then, as his own caught them, almost crushed them:

"Oh, it was your letter that ended all for me, Louis! It settled every doubt I had. I *knew* then—you darling!"

She bent and touched his hands with her lips, then lifted her sweet, untroubled gaze to his:

"I had been away from you so long, so long. And the time was approaching for me to decide, and I didn't know what was best for us, any more than when I went away. And *then!*—your letter came!"

She shook her head, slowly:

"I don't know what I might have decided if you never had written that letter to me; probably I would have come back to you anyway. I think so; I can't think of my doing anything else: though I *might* have decided—against myself. But as soon as I read your letter I *knew*, Louis. . . . And I am here."

He said with drawn lips quivering:

"Did you read in that letter one single word of cowardly appeal?—one infamous word of self? If you did, I wrote in vain."

"It was because I read nothing in it of self that I made up my mind, Louis." She stepped nearer. "Why are you so dreadfully pale and worn? Your face is so haggard—so terrible——"

She laid one hand on his shoulder, looking up at

511

him; then she smoothed his forehead and hair, lightly.

"As though I could ever live without you," she said under her breath. Then she laughed, releasing her hands, and went over to the dresser where there was a mirror.

"I have come, at one in the morning, to pay you a call," she said, withdrawing the long pins from her hat and taking it off. "Later I should like a cup of chocolate, please. . . . Oh, there is Gladys! You sweet thing!" she cried softly, kneeling to embrace the cat who came silently into the room, tail waving aloft in gentle greeting.

The girl lifted Gladys onto the bed and rolled her over into a fluffy ball and rubbed her cheeks and her ears until her furry toes curled, and her loud and grateful purring filled the room.

Valerie, seated sideways on the edge of the bed, looked up at Neville, laughing:

"I *must* tell you about Sam and Hélène," she said. "They are too funny! Hélène was furious because Sam wrote her a letter saying that he intended to marry her but had not the courage to notify her, personally, of his decision; and Hélène was wild, and wrote him that he might save himself further trouble in the matter. And they've been telephoning to each other at intervals all day, and Sam is so afraid of her that he dare not go to see her; and Hélène was in tears when I saw her —and I *think* it was because she was afraid Sam wouldn't come and resume the quarrel where she could manage it and him more satisfactorily."

She threw back her head and laughed at the recollection, stroking Gladys the while:

"It will come out all right, of course," she added, her eyes full of laughter; "she's been in love with Sam ever since he broke a Ming jar and almost died of fright. But isn't it funny, Louis?—the way people fall in love, and their various manners of informing each other!"

He was trying to smile, but the gray constraint in his face made it only an effort. Valerie pretended not to notice it, and she rattled on gaily, detailing her small budget of gossip and caressing Gladys—behaving as irresponsibly and as capriciously as though her heart were not singing a ceaseless hymn of happiness too deep, too thankful to utter by word or look.

"Dear little Rita," she exclaimed, suddenly and tenderly solemn—"I saw her the morning of the day she departed with John. And first of all I asked about you of course—you spoiled thing!—and then I asked about John. And we put our arms around each other and had a good, old-fashioned cry. . . . But—*don't* you think he is going to get well, Louis?"

"Sam's brother—Billy Ogilvy—wrote me that he would always have to live in Arizona. He *can* live there. But the East would be death to him."

"Can't he ever come back?" she asked pitifully.

"No, dear."

"But—but what will Rita do?"

He said: "I think that will depend on Rita. I think it depends on her already."

"Why?" she asked, wide-eyed. "Do you believe that John cares for her?"

"I know he does. . . . And I haven't much doubt that he wants to marry her."

" Do you think so? Oh, Louis—if that is true, what a heavenly future for Rita! "

" Heavenly? Out in that scorching desert? "

" Do you think she'd care *where* she was? Kelly, you're ridiculous! "

" Do you believe that any woman could stand that for the rest of her life, Valerie? "

She smiled, head lowered, fondling the cat who had gone ecstatically to sleep.

She said, still smiling: " If a girl is loved she endures some things; if she loves she endures more. But to a girl who is loved, and who loves, nothing else matters. . . . And it would be that way with Rita "—she lifted her eyes—" as it is with me."

He was standing beside her now; she made room on the side of the bed for him with a little gesture of invitation:

" People who die for each other are less admirable than people who live for each other. The latter requires the higher type of courage. . . . If I go out of your life I am like a dead person to you—a little worse in fact. Besides, I've shown the white feather and run away. That's a cowardly solution of a problem, isn't it? "

" Am I a coward if I decide to stand back and give you a chance? "

" You haven't decided to do it," she said cheerfully, lifting the somnolent cat and hugging it.

" I'm afraid I have, dear."

" Why? "

" You read my letter? "

" Yes and kissed every line in it."

He retained sufficient self-control to keep his hands

514

off her—but that was all; and her eyes, which were looking into his, grew serious and beautiful.

"I love you so," she breathed.

"I love you, Valerie."

"Yes. . . . I know it. . . . I know you do. . . . " She sat musing a moment, then: "And I thought that I knew what it was to love, before you wrote that letter." She shook her head, murmuring something to herself. Then the swift smile curved her lips again, she dumped Gladys out of her lap without ceremony, and leaned her shoulder on Neville's, resting her cheek lightly against his:

"It doesn't seem possible that the problem of life has really been solved for us, Louis. I can scarcely realise it—scarcely understand what this heavenly relief means—this utterly blissful relaxation and untroubled confidence. There isn't anything in the world that can harm me, now; is there?"

"Nothing."

"Nor my soul?"

"It has always been beyond danger."

"There are those who might tell me differently."

"Let them talk. I *know*."

"Do you?—you darling!" Her soft, fragrant mouth touched his cheek, lingered, then she laughed to herself for the very happiness of living.

"Isn't it wonderful how a word sometimes shatters the fixed ideas that a girl has arrived at through prayer and fasting? I am beginning to think that no real intelligence can remain very long welded to any one fixed belief."

"What do you mean, Valerie?" She rested her

head on his shoulder and sat considering, eyes remote; then her white fingers crept into his:

"We won't talk about it now. I was wrong in some ways. You or common sense—or something—opened my eyes. . . . But we won't talk about it now. . . . Because there are still perplexities—some few. . . . We'll go over them together—and arrange matters—somehow."

"What matters?"

But she placed a soft hand over his lips, imposing silence, and drew his arm around her with a little sigh of content.

Presently she said: "Have you noticed my gown? I made it."

He smiled and bent forward to look.

"I made *everything* that I am wearing—except the shoes and stockings. But they are perfectly new. . . . I wanted to come to you—perfectly new. There was a Valerie who didn't really love you. She thought she did, but she didn't. . . . So I left her behind when I came—left everything about her behind me. I am all new, Louis. . . . Are you afraid to love me?"

He drew her closer; she turned, partly, and put both arms around his neck, and their lips touched and clung.

Then, a little pale, she drew away from him, a vague smile tremulous on her lips. The confused sweetness of her eyes held him breathless with their enchantment; the faint fragrance of her dazed him.

In silence she bent her head, remained curbed, motionless for a few moments, then slowly lifted her eyes to his.

"How much do you want me, Louis?"

"You know."

"Enough to—give me up?"

His lips stiffened and refused at first, then:

"Yes," they motioned. And she saw the word they formed.

"I knew it," she breathed; "I only wanted to hear you say it again. . . . I don't know why I'm crying;— do you? . . . What a perfect ninny a girl can be when she tries to. . . . *All* over your collar, too. . . . And now you're what Mr. Mantalini would call 'demned moist and unpleasant!' . . . I—I don't want to— s-sob—this way! I do-don't wish to . . . M-make me stop, Louis! . . . I'd like a handkerchief—any-thing—give me Gladys and I'll staunch my tears on her!"

She slipped from the bed's edge to the floor, and stood with her back toward him. Then she glanced sideways at the mirror to inspect her nose.

"Thank goodness *that* isn't red," she said gaily. . . . "Kelly, I'm hungry. . . . I've fasted since dawn— on this day—because I wanted to break bread with you on the first day of our new life together."

He looked at her, appalled, but she laughed and went into the studio. There was a beautiful old side-board there always well stocked.

He turned on the lights, brought peaches and mel-ons and strawberries and milk from the ice-chest, and found her already preparing chocolate over the electric grill and buttering immense slices of peasant bread.

"It's after two o'clock," she said, delighted. "Isn't this divinely silly? I wonder if there happens to be any salad in the ice-chest?"

"Cold chicken, too," he nodded, watching her set the table.

She glanced at him over her shoulder from time to time:

"Louis, are you going to enjoy all this? *All* of it? You—somehow—don't look entirely happy——"

"I am. . . . All I wanted was to see you—hear your voice. . . . I shall be contented now."

"With just a view of me, and the sound of my voice?"

"You know there is—nothing more for us."

"I know nothing of the kind. The idea! And don't you dare struggle and kick and scream when I kiss you. Do you hear me, Louis?"

He laughed and watched her as she went swiftly and gracefully about the table arrangement, glancing up at him from moment to moment.

"The idea," she repeated, indignantly. "I guess I'll kiss you when I choose to. You are not in holy orders, are you? You haven't made any particular vows, have you——?"

"One."

She halted, looked at him, then went on with her labours, a delicate colour flushing face and neck.

"Where in the world is that salad, Louis? A hungry girl asks you! Don't drive me to desperation——"

"Are we going to have coffee?"

"No, it will keep us awake all night! I believe you *are* bent on my destruction." And, as she hovered over the table, she hummed the latest popular summer-roof ballad:

"'Stand back! Go 'way!
    I can no longer stay
        Although you are a Marquis or a Earl!
    You may tempt the upper classes
    With your villainous demi-tasses
    But ——
    Heaven will protect the Working Girl!'"

At length everything was ready. He had placed
two chairs opposite one another, but she wouldn't have
it, and made him lug up a bench, lay a cushion on it,
and sit beside her.

They behaved foolishly; she fed him strawberries
at intervals, discreetly, on a fork—and otherwise.

"Think of it! Fruit—at three in the morning,
Louis! I hope Heaven will protect *this* working girl.
. . . No, dear, I'd rather not have any champagne.
. . . You forget that this is a brand-new girl you're
supping with. . . . And, for reasons of her own—perhaps as an example to you—there is never again to be
anything like that—not even a cigarette."

"Nonsense——"

"Oh, it's on account of my voice, not my morals,
goose! I have rather a nice voice you know, and, if
we can afford it, it would be a jolly good idea to have
it cultivated. . . . Isn't this melon divine! What fun,
Louis! . . . I believe you *are* a little happier. That
crease between your eyes has quite disappeared—
There! Don't dare let it come back! It has no business there I tell you. I *know* it hasn't—and you must
trust my word. Will you?"

She leaned swiftly toward him, placed both hands
on his shoulders.

"You've a perfectly new girl to deal with," she said, looking him in the eyes;—"a miracle of meekness and patience that is rather certain to turn into a dreadful, frowsy old hausfrau some day. But that's the kind you wanted. . . . It's none of my doings——"

"Valerie!"

"What?"

"You darling!—do you mean——"

She closed his lips with hers.

"Silence," she said; "we have plenty to talk over before the hour arrives for me to be a door-mat. I *won't* be a door-mat when I'm trying to be happy over a perfectly good supper! . . . Besides I want to torture you while there's still time. I want to make you miserable by reminding you how disgracefully unmoral we are, here in your studio together at three in the morning——" She stretched out a slim, white ringless hand, and lifted the third finger for his inspection:

"Not a sign of a ring! Shame!" She turned her pretty, daring face to his, eyes sparkling with audacity:

"Besides, I'm not going back to-night."

He said tranquilly: "I should think not."

"I mean it, Kelly, I simply won't go. And you may ring up the police and every ambulance in town— and the fire department——"

"I've done it," he said, "but the fire department refuses to put you out. . . . You don't mean to say you've finished!—after fasting all day like a little idiot," he exclaimed as she sprang to her feet and pushed away her chair.

"I have. I am *not* an anaconda!" . . . She passed swiftly into the outer room where her own toilet necessaries were always ready, and presently came back,

leisurely, her hands behind her back, sauntering toward him with a provoking smile edging her lips:

" You may retire when you like, Kelly, and tie your red cotton night-cap under your chin. *I* shall sit up for the sun. It's due in about an hour, you know."

" Nonsense," he said. " We'll both be dead in the morning."

" You offer me your guest-room? " she said in pretence of surprise. " How *very* nice of you, Mr. Neville. I—ah—will condescend to occupy it—for this evening only—" Her eyes brightened into laughter: " Oh, isn't it delicious, Louis! Isn't it perfectly heavenly to *know* that we are utterly and absolutely all right, —and to know that the world outside would be perfectly certain that we are not? What a darling you are! "

Still holding her hands behind her back she bent forward and touched her lips to his, daintily, fastidious in the light contact.

" Where is that picture of ' Womanhood '? " she asked.

He drew out the easel, adjusting the canvas to the light, and rolled a big chair up in front of it.

" Please sit there," she said; and seated herself on the padded arm, still keeping her hands behind her back.

" Are you concealing anything from me? " he asked.

" Never mind. I want to look at your picture," she added slowly as her eyes fell upon the canvas.

Minute after minute she sat there in silence, neither stirring nor offering comment. And after a long time he moved restlessly in the depths of the chair beside her.

Then she turned and looked down at him:

"Yes," she said, "it is really great. . . . And, *somehow*, I am lonely. Take me, Louis."

He drew her into his arms. She lay very silent against his breast for a while, and at last raised her curiously troubled eyes.

"You are going to be a very, very great painter, aren't you, Louis?"

He laughed and kissed her, watching her face.

"Don't be too great—so great that I shall feel too —too lonely," she whispered.

Then his eyes fell upon the ring which he had given her—and which she had gently put aside. She was wearing it on her betrothal finger.

"Where did you—find it?" he said unsteadily.

"In its box on your dresser."

"Do you realise what it means?"

"Yes. . . . And I am wearing it."

"Valerie!"

Her head nestled closer:

"Because I am going to marry you, Louis. . . . You were right. . . . If I fail, as your wife, to win my way in your world, then it will be because I have attempted the impossible. Which is no crime. . . . Who was it said 'Not failure, but low aim is crime'?"

She sighed, nestling closer like a child seeking rest:

"I am not coward enough to run away from you and destiny. . . . And if I stay, only two ways remain. . . . And the lawful is the better for us both. . . ." She laid her flushed cheek against his: "Because," she said dreamily, "there is one thing of which I never thought—children. . . . And I don't, perhaps, exactly understand, but I realise that—such things have happened;—and that it could happen to—us."

She lay silent for a while, her fingers restless on his shoulder; then she spoke again in the same dreamy voice of a half-awakened child:

"Each for the other's sake is not enough. It must be broader, wider, more generous . . . it must be for the sake of all. . . . I have learned this. . . . We can learn it better together. . . . Louis, can you guess what I did the day your letter came to me at Estwich?"

"What did you do, my darling?"

"I went to Ashuelyn."

"What?"

"Yes, dear. If it had not been for your letter which I could feel against my breast I should have been frightened. . . . Because all your family were together under the pergola. . . . As it was I could scarcely speak; I gave your mother the letter, and when she had read it and your father and your sister had read it, I asked them what I was to do.

"It was so strange and still there under the pergola; and I scarcely knew what I was saying—and I didn't realise that there were tears in my eyes—until I saw them in your mother's, too.

"Louis! Louis! I wonder if she can really ever care for me!—she was so good—so sweet to me. . . . And Mrs. Collis took me away to her own room—after your father had shaken hands with me—very stiffly but I think kindly—and I behaved very badly, dear—and your sister let me cry—all that I needed to."

She said nothing more for a while, resting in his arms, dark eyes fixed on space. Then:

"They asked me to remain; your brother-in-law is a dear!—but I still had a long day of self-examination before me. Your father and mother walked with me to the gate. Your mother kissed me."

His eyes, blinded by tears, scarcely saw her; and she turned her head and smiled at him.

" What they said to me was very sweet and patient, Louis. . . . I believe—I sometimes believe that I may, in time, win more than their consent. I believe that, some day, they will care to think of me as your wife— and think of me as such, kindly, without regret for what might have been if I had never known you."

CHAPTER XVIII

Hélène d'Enver had gone back to the country, and Ogilvy dared not pursue her thither.

From her fastness at Estwich she defied him in letters, but every letter of hers seemed to leave some loophole open for further argument, and Ogilvy replied valiantly from a perfectly safe distance, vowing that he meant to marry her some day in spite of herself and threatening to go up and tell her so to her face, until she became bored to death waiting for him to fulfil this threat.

"There's a perfectly good inn here," she wrote,— "for of course, under the circumstances, you would scarcely have the impudence to expect the hospitality of my own roof. But if you are determined to have a final 'No' for your answer, I am entirely competent to give it to you by word of mouth——"

"And such a distractingly, lovely mouth," sighed Ogilvy, perusing the letter in his studio. He whistled a slow waltz, thoughtfully, and as slowly and solemnly kept step to it, turning round and round, buried in deepest reflection. He had a habit of doing this when profoundly perplexed.

Annan discovered him waltzing mournfully all by himself:

"What's up?" he inquired cheerfully.

"It's all up, I suppose."

527

" To Estwich? "

" When? " inquired Annan, sceptically.

" Now!—b' jinks! "

" Have *you* sufficient nerve, *this* time? "

" Watch me. "

And he dragged out a suit-case and began wildly throwing articles of toilet and apparel into it.

" Come on, Harry! " he shouted, hurling a pair of tennis shoes at the suit-case; " I've got to go while I'm excited or I'll never budge! "

But when, ten minutes later, Annan arrived, suit-case in hand, ready for love's journey, he could scarcely contrive to kick and drag Sam into the elevator, and, later, into a taxicab.

Ogilvy sat there alternately shivering and attempting to invent imperative engagements in town which he had just remembered, but Annan said angrily:

" No, you don't. This makes the seventh time I've started with you for Estwich, and I'm going to put it through or perish in a hand-to-hand conflict with you. "

And he started for the train, dragging Sam with him, talking angrily all the time.

He talked all the way to Estwich, too, partly to re-assure Ogilvy and give him no time for terrified reflection, partly because he liked to talk. And when they arrived at the Estwich Arms he shoved Ogilvy into a room, locked the door, and went away to telephone to the Countess d'Enver.

" Yes? " she inquired sweetly, " who is it? "

" Me, " replied Annan, regardless of an unpopular grammatical convention. " I'm here with Ogilvy. May we come to tea? "

" Is Mr. Ogilvy *here?* "

" Yes, here at the Estwich Arms. May I—er—may *he* bring *me* over to call on you? "

" Y-yes. Oh, with pleasure, Mr. Annan. . . . When may I expect hi—you? "

" In about ten minutes," replied Annan firmly.

Then he went back and looked into Ogilvy's room. Sam was seated, his head clasped in his hands.

" I thought you *might* tear up your sheets and let yourself out of the window," said Annan sarcastically. " You're a fine specimen! Why you're actually lantern-jawed with fright. But I don't care! Come on; we're expected to tea! Get into your white flannels and pretty blue coat and put on your dinkey rah-rah, and follow me. Or, by heaven!—I'll do murder right now! "

Ogilvy's knees wavered as they entered the gateway.

" Go on! " hissed Annan, giving him a violent shove.

Then, to Ogilvy, came that desperate and hysterical courage that comes to those whose terrors have at last infuriated them.

" By jinks! " he said with an unearthly smile, " I *will* come on! "

And he did, straight through the door and into the pretty living room where Hélène d'Enver rose in some slight consternation to receive this astonishingly pale and rather desperate-faced young man.

" Harry," said Ogilvy, calmly retaining Hélène's hand, " you go and play around the yard for a few moments. I have something to tell the Countess d'Enver; and then we'll all have tea."

" Mr. Ogilvy! " she said, amazed.

But Annan had already vanished; and she looked into a pair of steady eyes that suddenly made her quail.

" Hélène," he said, " I really do love you."

"'I am scared blue. That's why I'm holding on to your hand so desperately.'"

"Please——"

"No! I love you! Are you going to let me?"

"I—how on earth—what a perfectly senseless——"

"I know it. I'm half senseless from fright. Yes, I am, Hélène! Now! here! at this very minute, I am

531

"Oh!" said Hélène with a distressed glance at Annan.

"He's one, too," observed her affianced, coolly nodding toward Annan. "We're a sickening lot, Hélène —until some charming and genuine person like you comes along to jounce us out of our smiling and imbecile self-absorption."

"I," said Annan gravely, "am probably the most frightful snob that ever wandered, in a moment of temporary aberration, north of lower Fifth Avenue."

"I'm worse," observed Sam gloomily. "Help us, Hélène, toward loftier aspirations. Be our little uplift girl——"

"You silly things!" she said indignantly.

Later two riders passed the house, Cameron and Stephanie Swift, who saluted Hélène most cordially, and waved airy recognition to the two men.

"More snobs," commented Sam.

"They are very delightful people!" retorted Hélène hotly.

"Most snobs are when they like you."

"Sam! I won't have you express such sentiments!"

He bent nearer to her:

"Dearest, I never had any sentiments except for you. And only the inconvenient propinquity of that man Annan prevents me from expressing them."

"Please, Sam——"

"Don't be afraid; I won't. He wouldn't care;— but I won't. . . . Hello! Why look who's here!" he exclaimed, rising. "Why it's the great god Kelly and little Sunshine!"—as Neville and Valerie sprang out of Mrs. Collis's touring car and came up the walk.

sented to render me eternally and supremely happy; because if I tried to express to them that delirious fact I'd end by standing on my head in the grass——"

"You dear!" whispered Valerie, holding tightly to Hélène's hands.

"Isn't it dreadful?" murmured Hélène, turning her blue eyes on the man who never would grow old enough to grow up. "I had no such intention, I can assure you; and I don't even understand myself yet."

"Don't you?" said Valerie, laughing tenderly;— "then you are like all other women. What is the use of our ever trying to understand ourselves?"

Hélène laughed, too:

"No use, dear. Leave it to men who say *they* understand us. It's a mercy somebody does."

"Isn't it," nodded Valerie; and they kissed each other, laughing.

"My goodness, it's like the embrace of the two augurs!" said Ogilvy. "They're laughing at *us*, Kelly! —at you, and me and Harry!—and at man in general! —innocent man!—so charmingly and guilelessly symbolised by us! Stop it, Hélène! You make me shiver. You'll frighten Annan so that he'll *never* marry if you and Valerie laugh that way at each other."

"I wonder," said Hélène, quieting him with a fair hand laid lightly on his sleeve, "whether you all would remain and dine with me this evening—just as you are I mean;—and I won't dress——"

"I insist *proh pudeur*," muttered Sam. "I can't countenance any such saturnalia——"

"Oh, Sam, do be quiet, dear—" She caught herself up with a blush, and everybody smiled.

"What do we care!" said Sam. "I'm tired of con-

535

TITLES SELECTED FROM
GROSSET & DUNLAP'S LIST

A CERTAIN RICH MAN. By William Allen White.

A vivid, startling portrayal of one man's financial greed, its wide spreading power, its action in Wall Street, and its effect on the three women most intimately in his life. A splendid, entertaining American novel.

IN OUR TOWN. By William Allen White. Illustrated by F. R. Gruger and W. Glackens.

Made up of the observations of a keen newspaper editor, involving the town millionaire, the smart set, the literary set, the bohemian set, and many others. All humorously related and sure to hold the attention.

NATHAN BURKE. By Mary S. Watts.

The story of an ambitious, backwoods Ohio boy who rose to prominence. Everyday humor of American rustic life permeates the book.

THE HIGH HAND. By Jacques Futrelle. Illustrated by Will Grefe.

A splendid story of the political game, with a son of the soil on the one side, and a "kid glove" politician on the other. A pretty girl, interested in both men, is the chief figure.

THE BACKWOODSMEN. By Charles G. D. Roberts. Illustrated.

Realistic stories of men and women living midst the savage beauty of the wilderness. Human nature at its best and worst is well protrayed.

YELLOWSTONE NIGHTS. By Herbert Quick.

A jolly company of six artists, writers and other clever folks take a trip through the National Park, and tell stories around camp fire at night. Brilliantly clever and original.

THE PROFESSOR'S MYSTERY. By Wells Hastings and Brian Hooker. Illustrated by Hanson Booth.

A young college professor, missing his steamer for Europe, has a romantic meeting with a pretty girl, escorts her home, and is enveloped in a big mystery.

GROSSET & DUNLAP, 526 WEST 26th ST., NEW YORK

The Master's Violin

By MYRTLE REED

A Love Story, with a musical atmosphere. A picturesque, old German virtuoso is the reverent possessor of a genuine Cremona. He consents to take as his pupil a handsome youth who proves to have an aptitude for technique, but not the soul of the artist. The youth has led the happy, careless life of a modern, well-to-do young American, and he cannot, with his meagre past, express the love, the longing, the passion and the tragedies of life and its happy phases as can the master who has lived life in all its fulness. But a girl comes into his existence, a beautiful bit of human driftwood that his aunt had taken into her heart and home; and through his passionate love for her, he learns the lessons that life has to give—and his soul awakens.

Founded on a fact well known among artists, but not often recognized or discussed.

If you have not read "LAVENDER AND OLD LACE" by the same author, you have a double pleasure in store—for these two books show Myrtle Reed in her most delightful, fascinating vein—indeed they may be considered as masterpieces of compelling interest.

GROSSET & DUNLAP, Publishers, NEW YORK

The Prodigal Judge

By VAUGHAN KESTER

This great novel—probably the most popular book in this country to-day—is as human as a story from the pen of that great master of "immortal laughter and immortal tears," Charles Dickens.

The Prodigal Judge is a shabby outcast, a tavern hanger-on, a genial wayfarer who tarries longest where the inn is most hospitable, yet with that suavity, that distinctive politeness and that saving grace of humor peculiar to the American man. He has his own code of morals—very exalted ones—but honors them in the breach rather than in the observance.

Clinging to the Judge closer than a brother, is Solomon Mahaffy—fallible and failing like the rest of us, but with a sublime capacity for friendship; and closer still, perhaps, clings little Hannibal, a boy about whose parentage nothing is known until the end of the story. Hannibal is charmed into tolerance of the Judge's picturesque vices, while Miss Betty, lovely and capricious, is charmed into placing all her affairs, both material and sentimental, in the hands of this delightful old vagabond.

The Judge will be a fixed star in the firmament of fictional characters as surely as David Harum or Col. Sellers. He is a source of infinite delight, while this story of Mr. Kester's is one of the finest examples of American literary craftmanship.

GROSSET & DUNLAP, 526 WEST 26th ST., NEW YORK

GROSSET & DUNLAP'S
DRAMATIZED NOVELS

Original, sincere and courageous—often amusing—the kind that are making theatrical history.

MADAME X. By Alexandre Bisson and J. W. McConaughy. Illustrated with scenes from the play.

A beautiful Parisienne became an outcast because her husband would not forgive an error of her youth. Her love for her son is the great final influence in her career. A tremendous dramatic success.

THE GARDEN OF ALLAH. By Robert Hichens.

An unconventional English woman and an inscrutable stranger meet and love in an oasis of the Sahara. Staged this season with magnificent cast and gorgeous properties.

THE PRINCE OF INDIA. By Lew. Wallace.

A glowing romance of the Byzantine Empire, presenting with extraordinary power the siege of Constantinople, and lighting its tragedy with the warm underglow of an Oriental romance. As a play it is a great dramatic spectacle.

TESS OF THE STORM COUNTRY. By Grace Miller White. Illust. by Howard Chandler Christy.

A girl from the dregs of society, loves a young Cornell University student, and it works startling changes in her life and the lives of those about her. The dramatic version is one of the sensations of the season.

YOUNG WALLINGFORD. By George Randolph Chester. Illust. by F. R. Gruger and Henry Raleigh.

A series of clever swindles conducted by a cheerful young man, each of which is just on the safe side of a State's prison offence. As "Get-Rich-Quick Wallingford," it is probably the most amusing expose of money manipulation ever seen on the stage.

THE INTRUSION OF JIMMY. By P. G. Wodehouse. Illustrations by Will Grefe.

Social and club life in London and New York, an amateur burglary adventure and a love story. Dramatized under the title of "A Gentleman of Leisure," it furnishes hours of laughter to the play-goers.

GROSSET & DUNLAP, 526 WEST 26th ST., NEW YORK

THE NOVELS OF
STEWART EDWARD WHITE

THE RULES OF THE GAME. Illustrated by Lajaren A. Hiller

The romance of the son of "The Riverman." The young college hero goes into the lumber camp, is antagonized by "graft" and comes into the romance of his life.

ARIZONA NIGHTS. Illus. and cover inlay by N. C. Wyeth.

A series of spirited tales emphasizing some phases of the life of the ranch, plains and desert. A masterpiece.

THE BLAZED TRAIL. With illustrations by Thomas Fogarty.

A wholesome story with gleams of humor, telling of a young man who blazed his way to fortune through the heart of the Michigan pines.

THE CLAIM JUMPERS. A Romance.

The tenderfoot manager of a mine in a lonesome gulch of the Black Hills has a hard time of it, but "wins out" in more ways than one.

CONJUROR'S HOUSE. Illustrated Theatrical Edition.

Dramatized under the title of "The Call of the North."

"Conjuror's House is a Hudson Bay trading post where the head factor is the absolute lord. A young fellow risked his life and won a bride on this forbidden land.

THE MAGIC FOREST. A Modern Fairy Tale. Illustrated.

The sympathetic way in which the children of the wild and their life is treated could only belong to one who is in love with the forest and open air. Based on fact.

THE RIVERMAN. Illus. by N. C. Wyeth and C. Underwood.

The story of a man's fight against a river and of a struggle between honesty and grit on the one side, and dishonesty and shrewdness on the other.

THE SILENT PLACES. Illustrations by Philip R. Goodwin.

The wonders of the northern forests, the heights of feminine devotion, and masculine power, the intelligence of the Caucasian and the instinct of the Indian, are all finely drawn in this story.

THE WESTERNERS.

A story of the Black Hills that is justly placed among the best American novels. It portrays the life of the new West as no other book has done in recent years.

THE MYSTERY. In collaboration with Samuel Hopkins Adams

With illustrations by Will Crawford.

The disappearance of three successive crews from the stout ship "Laughing Lass" in mid-Pacific, is a mystery weird and inscrutable. In the solution, there is a story of the most exciting voyage that man ever undertook.

GROSSET & DUNLAP, 526 WEST 26th ST., NEW YORK

THE NOVELS OF
WINSTON CHURCHILL

Skillful in plot, dramatic in episode, powerful and original in climax.

MR. CREWE'S CAREER. Illus. by A.I. Keller and Kinneys.

A New England state is under the political domination of a railway and Mr. Crewe, a millionaire, seizes the moment when the cause of the people against corporation greed is being espoused by an ardent young attorney, to further his own interest in a political way, by taking up this cause.

The daughter of the railway president, with the sunny humor and shrewd common sense of the New England girl, plays no small part in the situation as well as in the life of the young attorney who stands so unflinchingly for clean politics

THE CROSSING. Illus. by S. Adamson and L. Baylis.

Describing the battle of Fort Moultrie and the British fleet in the harbor of Charleston, the blazing of the Kentucky wilderness, the expedition of Clark and his handful of dauntless followers in Illinois, the beginning of civilization along the Ohio and Mississippi, and the treasonable schemes builded against Washington and the Federal Government.

CONISTON. Illustrated by Florence Scovel Shinn.

A deft blending of love and politics distinguishes this book. The author has taken for his hero a New Englander, a crude man of the tannery, who rose to political prominence by his own powers, and then surrendered all for the love of a woman.

It is a sermon on civic righteousness, and a love story of a deep motive.

THE CELEBRITY. An Episode.

An inimitable bit of comedy describing an interchange of personalities between a celebrated author and a bicycle salesman of the most blatant type. The story is adorned with some character sketches more living than pen work. It is the purest, keenest fun—no such piece of humor has appeared for years: it is American to the core.

THE CRISIS. Illus. by Howard Chandler Christy.

A book that presents the great crisis in our national life with splendid power and with a sympathy, a sincerity, and a patriotism that are inspiring. The several scenes in the book in which Abraham Lincoln figures must be read in their entirety for they give a picture of that great, magnetic, lovable man, which has been drawn with evident affection and exceptional success.

GROSSET & DUNLAP, 526 WEST 26TH ST., NEW YORK